THE PAPACY AND TOTALITARIANISM
BETWEEN THE TWO WORLD WARS

MAJOR ISSUES IN HISTORY

Editor

C. WARREN HOLLISTER

University of California, Santa Barbara

THE PAPACY
AND TOTALITARIANISM
BETWEEN
THE TWO WORLD WARS

EDITED BY

Charles F. Delzell

Vanderbilt University

John Wiley & Sons, Inc.

New York • London • Sydney • Toronto

Library of Congress Cataloging in Publication Data:

Delzell, Charles F   comp.
    The Papacy and totalitarianism between the two World Wars.

    (Major issues in history)
    Bibliography: p.
    1. Papacy—History—20th century. 2. Papal documents. I. Title.

BX1389.D44   262′.13′0904   73-16419
ISBN 0-471-20638-5
ISBN 0-471-20639-3 (pbk.)
Printed in the United States of America

10 9 8 7 6 5 4 3 2 1

SERIES PREFACE

The reading program in a history survey course traditionally has consisted of a large two-volume textbook and, perhaps, a book of readings. This simple reading program requires few decisions and little imagination on the instructor's part, and tends to encourage in the student the virtue of careful memorization. Such programs are by no means things of the past, but they certainly do not represent the wave of the future.

The reading program in survey courses at many colleges and universities today is far more complex. At the risk of over-simplification, and allowing for many exceptions and overlaps, it can be divided into four categories: (1) textbook, (2) original source readings, (3) specialized historical essays and interpretive studies, and (4) historical problems.

After obtaining an overview of the course subject matter (textbook), sampling the original sources, and being exposed to selective examples of excellent modern historical writing (historical essays), the student can turn to the crucial task of weighing various possible interpretations of major historical issues. It is at this point that memory gives way to creative critical thought. The "problems approach," in other words, is the intellectual climax of a thoughtfully conceived reading program and is, indeed, the most characteristic of all approaches to historical pedagogy among the newer generation of college and university teachers.

The historical problems books currently available are many and varied. Why add to this information explosion? Because the Wiley Major Issues Series constitutes an endeavor to produce something new that will respond to pedagogical needs thus far unmet. First, it is a series of individual volumes—one per problem. Many good teachers would much prefer to select their own historical issues rather than be tied to an inflexible sequence of issues imposed by a publisher and bound together between two covers. Second, the Wiley Major Issues Series is based on the idea of approaching the significant problems of history through a deft interweaving of primary sources and secondary analysis, fused together by the skill of a scholar-editor. It is felt that the essence of a historical issue cannot be satisfactorily probed either by placing a body of undigested source materials into the hands of inexperienced students or by limiting these students to the controversial literature of modern scholars who debate the meaning of sources the student never sees. This series approaches historical problems by exposing students to both the finest historical thinking on the issue and some of the evidence on which this thinking is based. This synthetic approach should prove far more fruitful than either the raw-source approach or the exclusively second-hand approach, for it combines the advantages—and avoids the serious disadvantages—of both.

Finally, the editors of the individual volumes in the Major Issues Series have been chosen from among the ablest scholars in their fields. Rather than faceless referees, they are historians who know their issues from the inside and, in most instances, have themselves contributed significantly to the relevant scholarly literature. It has been the editorial policy of this series to permit the editor-scholars of the individual volumes the widest possible latitude both in formulating their topics and in organizing their materials. Their scholarly competence has been unquestioningly respected; they have been encouraged to approach the problems as they see fit. The titles and themes of the series volumes have been suggested in nearly every case by the scholar-editors themselves. The criteria have been (1) that the issue be of relevance to undergraduate lecture courses in history, and (2) that it be an issue which the scholar-editor knows thoroughly and in which he has done creative work. And, in general, the second criterion has been given precedence over the first. In short, the question "What are the significant historical issues today?" has been answered not by general editors or sales departments but by the scholar-teachers who are responsible for these volumes.

University of California,   *C. Warren Hollister*
Santa Barbara

CONTENTS

THE PAPACY AND TOTALITARIANISM
BETWEEN THE TWO WORLD WARS

INTRODUCTION

During the past decade controversy regarding the attitude of the Roman Catholic Church toward the totalitarian dictatorships of the era between the two world wars has become a burning issue. It was given new impetus by the appearance in 1963 of Rolf Hochhuth's play, *The Deputy (Der Stellvertreter)*, dealing with the wartime role of Pope Pius XII (1939–1958), Christ's "deputy" or vicar on earth. The play was extremely critical of Pius's alleged lack of moral concern for the plight of the Jews and his silence during Adolf Hitler's holocaust. Hochhuth attributed this behavior to a major flaw in Pius XII's moral character. The German playwright's serious charges provoked a torrent of emotional rebuttals and counterarguments, some of which are set forth in this problem book. They also caused the Holy See to hasten the publication of many relevant documents in the Vatican archives.

The debate soon broadened beyond the events of World War II to cover the preceding two decades as well, particularly with regard to the papacy's attitudes toward the totalitarian dictatorships. No one, of course, could find reason to accuse the Holy See of ever having been "soft" on the Communist regime that had emerged in Russia after the Bolshevik Revolution of November 1917 since the Church had maintained a consistently hostile and uncompromising attitude toward that atheistic ideology. But what about the papacy's position toward Benito Mussolini's Fascist government that came to power in Italy in October 1922 in the wake of postwar turbulence and fears on the part of many

1

property owners of a possible Marxian Socialist takeover? And toward Hitler's National Socialist regime that took control in depression-torn Germany in January 1933? Did Vatican policies contribute to the ease with which Mussolini and Hitler nailed down totalitarian dictatorships in both of these countries? Did the Vatican display a predilection for Mussolini's ideology of the radical right, so different in spirit from the liberal philosophy of the governments that had ruled Italy in the preceding half century in defiance of the Church? Did the papacy see a possibility of cultivating Mussolini in order to negotiate a settlement that would enhance the influence of the Roman Catholic Church in Italy? When Hitler came to power in Germany, did the Vatican object to disbanding the Catholic Center party? Was this necessary in order to facilitate the signing of a concordat with Hitler's Reich that would improve the Church's position in Germany as a whole?

The first two selections in this book attempt to place these and related problems in broad historical overview. They were written respectively by John P. McKnight, a liberal Presbyterian journalist, and by E. E. Y. Hales, an English Catholic historian. These passages afford the reader an interesting sample of many of the major criticisms of, and rationalizations for, the Vatican's policies with respect to the totalitarian dictatorships. McKnight is highly critical of Pius XI (1922–1939) for his hasty withdrawal of papal support from the recently founded and powerful Italian Popular party, which had become critical of Mussolini's Fascist party, and transferring it instead to "Catholic Action," a less politically independent movement of the Catholic laity. Hales, on the other hand, finds some justification for the Church's willingness to work out an accommodation with the Fascists. There can be little doubt, in any case, that this shift in the Vatican's political stance facilitated the secret negotiations that culminated, on February 11, 1929, in the signing of the famous Lateran pacts by Mussolini and Pietro Cardinal Gasparri, the Vatican secretary of state. These pacts were three in number: a treaty that recognized the legal existence of both the kingdom of Italy and the Vatican City, a concordat that governed relations between church and state and imposed upon the latter the Church's legislation in matters affecting marriage, and a financial agreement that made the Vatican a major bondholder of the Italian state. The pacts brought an end to almost sixty years of hostility between church and state in Italy. By these accords Mussolini attained enormous popularity not only among Catholics at home but throughout the world. Pius XI, who was often inclined to emotional exclamations, publicly extolled the Fascist *Duce* as "a man . . . whom Providence has caused us to meet!" Many anti-Fascists and anticlericals were not disposed to let his phrase be quickly forgotten.

Yet, as Hales and other writers have pointed out, this same pontiff was to become involved less than two years later in an acrimonious dispute with Mussolini over the status of Catholic Action vis-à-vis the single-party dictatorship and over the activities of Catholic youth groups that competed with Fascist youth organizations. In June 1931 Pius XI did not hesitate to send to the Italian bishops a blunt encyclical letter, *Non abbiamo bisogno* ("We have no need"), to be read from their pulpits. It sternly denounced the behavior of the Fascist dictatorship toward Catholic Action. Was the authoritarian-minded Church willing, however, to risk a possible collapse of the Lateran pacts it had signed with the would-be totalitarian Fascist state? The reader may consider this problem as he examines excerpts from the papal encyclical in the documentary section of this book.

In another important encyclical of 1931—*Quadragesimo anno* ("The fortieth year")—Pius XI took advantage of the opportunity provided by the anniversary of *Rerum novarum* (Pope Leo XIII's famous pronouncement in 1891 of Catholic thought regarding the proper social relationship of capital and labor) to update the Church's teaching in this sector. Among other things, he criticized certain features of Mussolini's much-advertised Corporative State that did not correspond to Catholic corporativist doctrines. The reader should recall that Mussolini's Corporative State was an inflated bureaucratic structure that sought to bring about class harmony by regimenting both labor and (to a much lesser degree) capital. It prohibited both strikes and lockouts, and it set up labor courts to arbitrate economic disputes. Organized slowly over many years, the Fascist Corporative State was inspired by both Catholic and syndicalist philosophies. The reader may properly ask himself just how deep seated were the

disagreements between Pius XI and Mussolini on corporativ-
ism. Excerpts from *Quadragesimo anno* are to be found in Part
IV of this book.

Within another year or two after that papal pronouncement
Germany was crowding Italy off the front of the Fascist political
stage. Adolf Hitler became German chancellor on January 30,
1933. His vice-chancellor was Franz von Papen, a prominent
Catholic politician. The votes of the Catholic Center party in the
Reichstag provided Hitler with the two-thirds majority he needed
to nail down the dictatorship. Did the Catholic leadership thereby bear grave responsibility for what was to happen? By June
1933 the Center party had been dissolved and a concordat
signed between the Third Reich and the Holy See. In these negotiations the Vatican was represented by its new Cardinal Secretary of State Eugenio Pacelli, six years later to become Pope
Pius XII.

The ink had scarcely dried on the German concordat of 1933
when Hitler made his racist policies toward the Jews clearer.
What was the nature of the papacy's response to Hitler's persecution of the Jews in Germany and, subsequently, to Mussolini's
in Italy when the *Duce* began to ape the *Fuehrer's* measures?
Pius XI's encyclical of March 1937, *Mit brennender Sorge*
("With burning anguish"), has often been cited as evidence of
the Vatican's moral revulsion for Hitler's racism. Portions of it
are printed in the documentary section. Did this encyclical criticize anti-Semitism per se? What role did Cardinal Pacelli play in
its drafting? Should special significance be attached to the fact
that Pius XI almost simultaneously denounced communism in
the encyclical, *Divini redemptoris*? Several well-informed observers have pointed out that in the months before his death in
February 1939, Pius XI showed increasing signs of disillusionment not only with Hitler's dictatorship but also with Mussolini's. The pontiff's death occurred the day before he was planning
to deliver an address on the tenth anniversary of the Lateran
pacts, a speech that would have been quite critical of Mussolini's
racist policies. Does this suggest that if the rather blunt Pius XI
had continued to be pope through the agonies of World War II,
he might have reacted to Hitler's massacre of the Jews more
forthrightly than his reticent successor, Pius XII?

Pius XII has been widely denounced for tending to immure himself behind walls of silence during the war, a stillness that was interrupted only occasionally by messages cast often in obscure, involuted language. What lay behind this wall of silence? Fear of Hitler's vengeance? Religious insensitivity toward non-Roman Catholics? Prudent but perhaps excessive concern for the Vatican's diplomatic role both present and future? Do you think that the Church either should or could have performed its moral mission more effectively than it did during the war years? Would outspokenly prophetic pronouncements or the hurling of thunderous anathemas and interdicts in the style of the Middle Ages have been in order? Or threats to repudiate the Church's concordat with the Third Reich? These are but a few of the questions that the reader may wish to weigh as he considers Pacelli's controversial pontificate. Although McKnight and Hales discuss some of these issues, the authors of the ensuing group of selections explore them in greater detail: Guenter Lewy, a political scientist of German Jewish background; John S. Conway, a Canadian historian of Roman Catholic faith; and Rolf Hochhuth, the playwright, in his radio interview with Patricia Marx.

In this connection, it may be pointed out that Pacelli was no stranger to Germany. During World War I he had been dispatched there on an important diplomatic mission for the Vatican. He was stationed at the Apostolic Nunciature in Munich in April 1919 when armed Spartacist Red Guards broke in. Pacelli insisted on facing them alone. His firm and dignified protest caused them to withdraw without violence. One critic has argued that this victory served as both a genuine shock and stimulant to Pacelli's nervous system and produced in him a kind of self-exaltation.[1] The reader may wish to ponder whether such an experience could have made Pacelli unduly sympathetic to German right-wing political forces, or whether it may have helped inspire his denunciations of Communist regimes after World War II. Pacelli's memory of the incident was apparently still vivid when, in response to a protest being delivered to him by Mussolini's ambassador to the Holy See in May 1940, he defiantly raised his

[1] Carlo Falconi, *The Silence of Pius XII*, trans. by Bernard Wall (Boston-Toronto: Little, Brown and Company, 1970), p. 85.

voice and declared: "Whatever may happen, We have absolutely nothing to be ashamed of, and We do not even fear deportation to a concentration camp! . . . We were not afraid of the revolvers pointed at Us once before; We are even less so this second time."[2]

The last two sections of the book focus on the question of whether World War II was, for the anti-Axis powers, a "just war." Was it proper for the Vatican to maintain a "hands-off" policy toward the belligerents? Saul A. Friedlaender's criticisms of Pius XII's actions need to be counter-balanced by the evidence set forth by Harold G. Deutsch regarding Pacelli's cooperation with German anti-Nazi conspirators in 1939 and 1940. What brought this collaboration to an end?

Should the pope have publicly expressed a moral judgment as to who was the aggressor? Is it likely that such a stand would have led the Axis dictators to cut off the Vatican from communication with the outside world? Might it have torpedoed any possibility for the Vatican to mediate the conflict? Would it have been inconsistent for Pius to condemn Hitler's Germany during the war and not also speak out against Stalin's Russia, which was an ally of the Anglo-Americans?

The proper delimitation of authority between church and state has been a persistent problem in the history of Christianity. To what extent was Pius XII willing to accept the authority of the state in the modern world? Does his encyclical, *Summi pontificatus,* issued a few weeks after the outbreak of the war, suggest any significant shift in political temperament on the part of the Roman Catholic Church in the twentieth century?

Finally, the reader should consider the allocution delivered by Pius XII to the Sacred College of Cardinals in Rome on June 2, 1945, less than a month after the defeat of Nazi Germany. What does it suggest may have been the true feelings of that pope toward National Socialism and the war?

[2] Secrétairerie d'État de sa Sainteté, *Actes et documents du Saint Siège relatifs à la Seconde Guerre Mondiale,* édités par Pierre Blet, Angelo Martini, Burkhart Schneider, Tome I: *Le Saint Siège et la guerre en Europe: Mars 1939—Août 1940* (Vatican City, 1965) , pp. 453–455; *cf.* Dino Alfieri, *Dictators Face to Face* (London, 1954) , pp. 15–17.

In the light of the various interpretations and documents presented in this book, can a satisfactory answer be rendered to the overall questions posed? If not, what additional types of evidence would be most helpful to the historian in making possible a balanced evaluation of the papacy's relationship to the totalitarian regimes between the two world wars?

PART ONE

The Papacy and the Dictatorships

John P. McKnight
The Papacy and Fascism

The selection that follows provides an overview from an unmistakably Protestant, liberal perspective of the Vatican's controversial relationships with Fascist Italy and Nazi Germany. John P. McKnight, who now lives in Florida, was formerly an Associated Press correspondent in Rome for the Los Angeles Mirror. While assigned there he became acquainted with American prelates in the Vatican Secretariat of State, the editors of the Vatican newspaper L'Osservatore Romano, *and had audiences with Pope Pius XII. He did subsequent research for the book in the library of the University of North Carolina at Chapel Hill. At the time he published this work, McKnight explained that it was his "chief purpose to study the impact and influence of the Roman Church and her papacy, . . . and especially of the present Pope [Pius XII], on our times. Thus I propose to examine their political, rather than their religious, aspects and effects, their temporal manifestations rather than the faith* qua *faith." Some Catholic reviewers contended that McKnight's account was not always well informed, but generally agreed that he sought to write without malice.*

Looking back on his own book from the perspective of the 1970s, Mr. McKnight has conceded that "events have dated some minor parts" of this selection, and that "the Vatican has moved perceptibly, if diffidently, toward accommodation with

SOURCE. *The Papacy: A New Appraisal* by John P. McKnight, pp. 274–296. Copyright © 1952 by John P. McKnight. Reprinted by permission of Holt, Rinehart and Winston, Inc.; Curtis Brown, Ltd., London; and Mr. John P. McKnight, 245 Second Avenue, North, Naples, Florida. Footnotes renumbered.

11

communism (as, indeed, the nature of communism itself has subtly altered). . . . [But] in the main, I think, the chapter stands up pretty well, even 20 years after."

An atavistic totalitarianism has arisen in our neurotic twentieth century to challenge liberal democracy, the dominant political philosophy of the nineteenth, at many places.

Fascist totalitarianism captured and lost two important Western countries: Italy and Germany. It still rules several lesser ones: Spain, Portugal, Argentina. It is tragicomically caricatured in others: the Dominican Republic.

Communist totalitarianism, having conquered backward Russia in World War I, has now—by Russian arms, Russian propaganda, Russian polity—been extended to several other Eastern countries: the most important, by the usual statistical measurements, is China.

We shall now consider the attitude of the popes toward this twentieth-century totalitarianism. Later, we shall take up their views on communism. Here, we are concerned with the papacy and fascism.

Fascist governments, while showing general family likenesses, have exhibited individual peculiarities. This has made for differences in the popes' approach to the several Fascist regimes. We have not space to consider these differences in detail. However, study of church-state relations in Fascist Italy, prototype of all the century's Fascist governments, will throw much light on over-all papal policy.

Some general considerations affecting this policy may be stated at the outset:

1. Rome favors governments that favor her, regardless of their form or of their political philosophy.

2. There is, however, an affinity, and so an initial attraction, between the authoritarian Roman Church and the totalitarian state.

3. Rulers of some modern totalitarian states, shrewd opportunists, have realized that to win the favor of the Church is to gain an initially useful ally (that may be discarded when no longer needed).

4. But the papacy and the true totalitarian state come finally

into conflict, because both compete for possession of the whole mind and heart and soul of men.

As Paul Blanshard points out, no pope has ever said, or will ever say, that he is Fascist (or democrat or Communist).[1] The Roman Church does not favor one political philosophy above another. She favors or opposes individual secular states; but she has no rule good for all times and places: her criteria are those of expedience. She does not inquire whether governments secure to men life, liberty, the pursuit of happiness; she asks only: does this or that government help or hamper the Catholic Church and her priesthood?

Anglican T. S. Eliot puts this policy on high theological ground: "To identify any particular form of government with Christianity is a dangerous error: for it confounds the permanent with the transitory, the absolute with the contingent."[2]

Professor Halecki, the Catholic historian, explains it thus: the Vatican does not "refuse the hand of peace of Mother Church to anyone who does not himself reject it"; it will "negotiate with any kind of government" that safeguards "the most vital elements of religious life."[3] Just so, novelist Bruce Marshall has his Father Smith say that the Church, "always aware that she must not unnecessarily give offense lest she lose souls for Almighty God," compacts "with heathen and heretical governments, that she may distribute the Bread of Life as widely as possible."[4] Pius XI was more blunt: he said that he would deal with the Devil if it would help the Church.[5]

Rome's politic approach to the state derives from her premises that the salvation of man's soul far outweighs his earthly well-being, that

"there is one thing that is worse than a million young men dying on the field of battle, and that is one old man dying in his bed in a state of final impenitence . . ."[6]

[1] Paul Blanshard, *American Freedom and Catholic Power* (Boston, 1949), pp. 240–241.

[2] T. S. Eliot, *The Idea of a Christian Society* (New York, 1940), p. 57.

[3] Oscar Halecki (with James F. Murray, Jr.), *Eugenio Pacelli: Pope of Peace* (London, 1954), p. 73.

[4] Bruce Marshall, *The World, the Flesh and Father Smith* (Armed Services Edition, by arrangement with Houghton Mifflin), pp. 186–187.

[5] Ernesto Buonaiuti, *Pio XII* (Rome, 1946), p. 99.

[6] Marshall, *op. cit.*, p. 187.

that the Roman Church alone can guarantee salvation, that it is hence the most important obligation of the state—its chief *raison d'être*—to aid her in that work, and that all states are good that do so aid her.

That, judged by secular standards, is opportunism: Rome resents the word, but, in this context, accepts the imputation.

If it is true that the papacy has for much of the last three decades favored Fascist governments, and still cherishes—albeit less enthusiastically—some flotsam from the Italo-German wreck, it is also true that as of today it regards with much approval the Western democracies.

There are several reasons for this change of front.

One is that the defeat of fascism leaves democracy dominant in the West—and the Vatican, now as always, sides with the winner.

A second reason is that democracy has replaced fascism as the barrier to dread communism.

A third is that Pope Pius XII, having personally observed democracy in action, has apparently accepted much of its philosophy as valid—the first pope to do so.

But the most important reason is this: Rome has belatedly perceived that totalitarianism (Fascist or Communist) however obsequiously helpful to church religion at the outset, must in the end deify the state and its ruler, develop its own *mystique*, myth, and mumbo-jumboism, its own exaltation of the irrational, and so become rival for man's religious devotion. And man, however polytheistic, rarely patronizes two pantheons.

In the first encyclical of his reign, Pius XII wrote:

"Once the authority of God and the sway of His law are denied . . . the civil authority . . . puts itself in the place of the Almighty and elevates the state or group into the last end of life, the supreme criterion of the moral and juridical order . . . ."[7]

All secular states, to some extent, govern by demanding devotion: this is called patriotism. But the totalitarian state carries this demand to extreme limits. Its very name implies that it seeks

[7] *Summi Pontificatus*, Oct. 20, 1939.

the *totality* of its subjects' allegiances—as Mussolini said, "Everything and everyone for the State." It cannot tolerate enclaves of doubt, of indifference, of divided loyalty: all must bow mind and heart, as well as knee.

Conflict between pope and totalitarian dictator comes about *not* because totalitarianism tramples man's freedoms: until recently, these freedoms have not weighed heavily in the papal scales. It comes about *not* because totalitarianism questions religion's social usefulness: the Vatican has able dialecticians to deal with such philosophical doubts. It comes about *not* because totalitarianism is inherently anticlerical,[8] *not* because the dictator fears hierarchical sabotage of his program (as he often does). Nor, finally, does conflict arise because the totalitarian state is (in some cases) neopagan, because its preaching and its practice are (in almost all cases) "explicitly, exquisitely anti-Christian."[9]

All these considerations have their influence. Still, Roman Church and totalitarian state come into conflict chiefly because it finally becomes clear to both that they are deadly rivals. The supply of potential converts and the techniques of proselytization being the same for secular and religious movements, the state must invade areas the Church claims as her own. Of these, the most important is the education of youth: both want to bend the twig. Battle is thereupon joined. And, since possession of power tempts irresistibly to employment of power, the state may at last use force against clerical pretensions.

"It may be asked why Pius XI, perceiving this, so long forbore to condemn Italian fascism. Jemolo offers the likeliest answer: Pius saw that, in the feverish early years of fascism, loyalties to the Duce were stronger than loyalties to the papacy; in an open breach, millions of Italians might have apostatized: there would even have been defections, Jemolo thinks, from clergy and episcopate.[10]

[8] Spain and Argentina are adventitious, perhaps temporary, exceptions; Portugal is *sui generis*.
[9] *Cf.* Buonaiuti, *op. cit.*, p. 43.
[10] Arturo Carlo Jemolo, *Chiesa e Stato in Italia durante l'ultimo cento anni* (Turin, 1948), p. 682. Throughout this chapter, I lean heavily on Jemolo, who offers the best short treatment of the church-state situation in Fascist Italy I have seen.

"Pius's indulgence 'embittered, scandalized, alienated' some Catholics, Jemolo says, but 'condemnation of Fascism, a struggle with the regime [that posed as] protector of the family, of [private] property, of the fatherland, of religion, would have scandalized a far greater number; . . . the . . . Church, placed in the dolorous alternative of scandalizing the ones or the others, acted wisely if it scandalized the fewer . . .' "[11]

If the Communist variety of totalitarianism has never merited anything but the Vatican's sharpest condemnation, that is because communism has from the start frankly proclaimed itself atheist, anti-Church, anti-pope.

Just so, it is not primarily the fact that democracy espouses man's freedoms that has latterly brought the popes to favor it: democracy appeals because nowadays, in most cases, it no longer aspires to enlist man's religious sentiments; it does not seek to monopolize his allegiances; it is content with part of them, as totalitarianism may never be.

"Democracy has, in the past, vied with religion for man's worship.

"Revolutionary France excited papal hostility because she symbolized the liberal constitutionalism that became Europe's 'new faith.' Popes and prelates detested America's frontier democracy partly because it was uncouth, partly because its inspiration was Protestant, but mostly because it inspired quasi-religious fervor: it was no accident that Leo XIII's denunciation of an 'American heresy' coincided with 'Manifest Destiny.' The popes' long recalcitrance before Italian unification was in part pique at loss of the papal domains, in part hatred of the new state's liberal tenets (and anticlericalism), but in large part also distrust of Mazzini's *Risorgimento* concept of the 'third' Italy's mission in the world—supply of an absent 'genuine and holy authority'—to rival Catholicism's 'mission.' "[12]

In the second quarter of the twentieth century, democracy lost

[11] Ibid., p. 685.
[12] See G. F. H. and J. Berkeley, *Italy in the Making* (Cambridge, Eng., 1932–40), Vol. I, pp. 13–14.

much of its onetime missionary drive. The slogan "Make the world safe for democracy" now gets only rueful, somewhat shame-faced smiles. Except for an occasional old-school American politico, the democratic "way of life" no longer has religious overtones. Not idealism, but the hard realities of power politics, justify the Marshall Plan, Point Four.

The United States has not sought spiritual and moral leader-ship in the West: it has been thrust upon her. She does not want to save the world: she tries to do so only because she begins to see that if the world goes smash so will she. Her approach to he-gemony is, uniquely in modern history, unattended by evangelis-tic ardor for remaking the world in her own image.

In other words, democracy does not now set itself up as an all-sufficient faith. It suggests itself to man as perhaps the best system yet devised under which—within the limitations of, and even because of, his imperfections—he may shape some reasona-bly satisfactory society. But it does not try to tell him (usually) what to think, what to believe: it merely offers him the *right* to think, to believe what he chooses; it does not specify the objects upon which his religious sentiments shall fasten: it lets him pick his own gods.

"The grievous implications of this are that, if it comes to a final test between democracy and communism or resurgent fas-cism (or militant Catholicism), democracy may be found want-ing. All else being equal, fanaticism carries the palm over toler-ance. Men crave gods, and die for them; and all the *isms* provide gods—communism the society, fascism the state and its dictator, Catholicism Jehovah and its subdivinities. But democracy, where it supplies gods, is at pains to point out that they have clay feet."

For that and for other reasons, the Catholic Church nowadays (as Pius XII has himself remarked) gets along very well under democracy.

If the Roman Church and her popes have come at last to op-pose totalitarian states because they compete for the devotion of their faithful, it is nevertheless true that they displayed an early fondness for fascism; and it is difficult to explain this without re-course to the theory that there exists an affinity between the two systems.

Blanshard quotes Count Coudenhove-Kalergi, onetime Catholic, thus:

"Catholicism is the fascist form of Christianity . . . Calvinism represents its democratic wing. The Catholic hierarchy rests fully and securely on the leadership principle with the infallible Pope in supreme command for a lifetime . . . Like the Fascist party, its priesthood becomes a medium for an undemocratic minority rule by a hierarchy. . . . Catholic nations follow fascist doctrines more willingly than Protestant nations, which are the main strongholds of democracy. . . . Democracy lays its stress on personal conscience; fascism on authority and obedience."[13]

Buonaiuti similarly explains the "instinctive acquiescence" of the Vatican Curia in nascent totalitarianism: he asks whether it

"did not constitute and represent, in substance, pure and simple transfer into the political and state field of criteria and methods, also brutally totalitarian, prevalent for centuries in the exercise of the ecclesiastical magisterium."[14]

That is perhaps too strongly put. In this day and age, the Roman Church is not avowedly totalitarian (although it has been in the past and may be again in the future). It is, however, authoritarian. And authoritarianism is evidently closer to totalitarianism than to democracy. This kinship may have begotten an initial sympathy.

Again, Rome, throughout history, has cherished the strong *homo novus* who will fight her battles. Constantine, Justinian, Pepin, Charlemagne, Otto the Great, their Catholic Majesties of Spain, the Hapsburgs, the Bourbons—all have served her well. It

---

[13] In *American Freedom and Catholic Power*, pp. 257–258. That Protestant nations are the bulwarks of freedom is also the thesis of Frederick Hoffet's *L'Impérialisme Protestant*, published in France in 1948. But, as we have seen, some Protestants now argue that the Lutheran separation of church and state may make Protestant churches unresistant to tyranny: predominantly Protestant Germany offered Hitler little more opposition than Catholic Italy Mussolini (although the resistance record of German churchmen, both Catholic and Protestant, is better than the Italians').

[14] Buonaiuti, *Pio XII*, p. 110.

was natural that Pius XI should look on Mussolini, on Hitler (briefly), on Salazar, on Franco as champions to put the modern infidels to the sword.

And the all-to-human Pope Ratti [Pius XI] doubtless shared with the generality of mankind the unreasoning admiration of bold, ruthless adventurers that makes so easy their way to power.

"Moreover, Mussolini's performance as a latter-day Caesar was, in the early acts, a pretty convincing one. Every year deposits in our minds its layer of memories, making those of the yesteryears harder to get at: we remember now the gross body hung upside down in the Milan gas station, like butchered beef, but we forget the flashing eye, the outthrust lips, the jutting jaw, the nude muscular torso of the early years; we recall now the universal opprobrium of the late thirties and forties, but we forget the universal acclaim of the twenties; we hear the biting invective of Churchill and Roosevelt, but we are deaf to the echoes of the great roar of 'Duce! Duce! Duce!'—that in the beginning rose spontaneously, without prodding from Fascist bullies.

"Indeed, it may be plausibly (if unfashionably) argued that Mussolini possessed all the requisites for greatness except greatness of heart and soul. It is often said now that the Predappio blacksmith's son was a *uomo qualunque*[15] who came to power solely because of the postwar disorder in Italy and the postwar mediocrity of Italy's politicians. Something of that may be true: it is an old argument whether the man makes the moment or the moment the man. But we need not deny Mussolini's extraordinary equipment for dictatorship: courage (as his World War I record shows); great personal magnetism; superb oratory; uncanny shrewdness; an almost miraculous feeling for public opinion; intuitive sense of the popular, the opportune. A *condottiere* he was, but one of the ablest.

"It is hardly surprising that Pius XI, the Italian prelacy, and the overwhelming majority of Italians fell under his spell."

There is still another reason for Pius XI's early tenderness for Mussolini and his Fascists: Pius recognized that they were

---

[15] "run–of–the–mill person" (*ed.*)

"faithless and lawless"; but he thought he could get along with them because they did not share "the villainous fetish of liberalism."[16]

"Perhaps there was needed [the old pope said after the signing of the Lateran Pacts] a man like the one Providence let us find; a man who would not have the concerns of the liberal school, for the men of which all those laws, all those ordinances . . . were so many fetishes and, exactly like fetishes, the uglier and more deformed the more untouchable and venerated."[17]

That is, Pius and Mussolini hated the same enemies; and there is perhaps no stronger bond.

"A movement [says Jemolo] that claimed to be a reaction not only against the socialists, not only against the liberals, but, looking still further [back], against Jacobins and Girondists, against the Encyclopaedists and the men of the Enlightenment, could hardly appear to Catholics as irreconcilable with their faith."[18]

The number one joint enemy, of course, was communism. In that war-ruined, debt-harried, restless, disillusioned Italy of the early twenties, communism found rich soil. Its rapid growth frightened pope, king, people. A "savior" much less plausible than Mussolini would have been welcomed by this nation weary of lockouts and strikes, fearful lest mounting violence become civil war, panic-stricken lest workers' occupation of factories prepare the way for sovietization.

These fears, the Vatican, whose initial denunciation of communism antedated the Communist Manifesto,[19] shared: fascism's promise to contain communism was as welcome in the twenties as democracy's in the forties and fifties; the Duce's alternative, "Rome or Moscow," fell sweetly on Vatican ears; in fact, Mussolini gone, the Vatican would take the slogan as its own, and find it no less useful.

[16] Carlo Sforza, *Contemporary Italy* (New York, 1944), p. 339.

[17] Speech to students of the University of the Sacred Heart, Feb. 13, 1929.

[18] Jemolo, *op. cit.*, pp. 598–599.

[19] Pius IX, encyclical, *Qui pluribus*, Nov. 9, 1846. The Communist Manifesto appeared in 1848.

A cloistered bibliophile snatched from the congenial work of classifying the Vatican Library's moldy tomes to diplomatic duty in turbulent postwar Poland and brief episcopal service in equally turbulent Milan, Achille Ratti came back to the quiet purlieus of the Apostolic Palace deeply distrustful of the disorderly processes of secular politics. Conversely, his life of scholarship had given him profound respect for the written word. As his cavalier way with Europe's new Christian Democrat movements would show, he was unwilling to entrust church-state relationships to the "uncertain equilibrium of parties": treaties "drafted in traditional form and foreseeing all cases" better suited his temperament—just as "one of those fine catalogues, of which he was so fond, seemed to him of more value . . . than the most accurate familiarity with books."[20]

Here was, perhaps, the psychological genesis of his "mania" for concordats that, in Buonaiuti's opinion, was the "incontrovertible sign of progressive decadence in the compelling power of the Roman Catholic magisterium."[21]

If in the twelfth century concordats had been useful to settle the great investiture controversies arising with the appearance of Catholic secular states, they were of little value in the twentieth, when few civil rulers were devoted sons of the Church, and when respect for treaties was everywhere at low ebb. Meditation on recent history (and, perhaps, more experience of the world) should have convinced Pius XI that no contract was better than its signers. He might well have pondered, too, a favorite saying of his predecessor: *Historia Concordatorum, historia dolorum* (the story of concordats is the story of sorrows) :[22] in the first

[20] Sforza, *op. cit.*, p. 339. An unnamed Roman newspaper quoted by Buonaiuti, 80, observed on Ratti's election that something "much better than the narrow-mindedness of a . . . paleographer shut up for decades in the corridors of the Ambrosian and Vatican [libraries]" was needed to restore the spirit of the Gospel in the world.

[21] Buonaiuti, *op. cit.*, p. 81. Of 18 concordats Pius XI negotiated, only the one with Italy is still fully operative.

[22] In Sforza, *op. cit.*, p. 334, p. 341, he relates that Cardinal Gasparri, returning to the Vatican after signing the 1929 agreements, saw two men fighting, and remarked to his secretary, "I wonder how long it has been since they signed a concordat."

half of the nineteenth century, "when relations with the Church were regulated by traditional jurisdictional agreements," the alliance of "throne and altar" had everywhere in Europe strengthened antipapal sentiment.[23] And thought should have persuaded Pius also that, though Vatican apologists might plead the contrary, concordats were popularly held to constitute Church approval of the civil signatories.

Nevertheless, Pope Ratti set himself from the outset to get concordats wherever he could.

Most eagerly desired, of course, was an agreement with Italy; from the start of his reign, Ratti evinced willingness to end the fifty-year-old "Roman question": at his election February 6, 1922, he came to the outer balcony of St. Peter's to impart the blessing *urbi et orbi* (to the city and to the world), the first pope since Pius IX to do so.

"By all accounts, the old differences with Italy could have been settled much earlier. The apolitical Pius X wanted to be 'the pope of conciliation'; lingering curial animosities, and want of the right man at the head of the Italian government, prevented.[24] After World War I, Benedict doubtless could have worked it out with Orlando, had the Sicilian premier not been so busy with the Paris peace talks. Nitti, Orlando's successor, was also eager for agreement; talks with Cardinal Gasparri opened up promising avenues; but the vicissitudes of politics too soon forced Nitti out. The perennial Giolitti, who for the fifth time succeeded to the premiership, believed it best for church and state 'to continue as in the past: two parallels that get on well together without ever coming into contact.' And Benedict's death canceled scheduled talks with the next premier, Bonomi."[25]

Ironically, it fell out that Pius XI signed with Mussolini— Mussolini the old atheist, anticlerical, Socialist, internationalist,

[23] Luigi Sturzo, *Italy and the Coming World* (New York, 1945), 115. Paul Blanshard, *Communism, Democracy, and Catholic Power* (Boston, 1951), 269, says the Holy See made 26 important agreements in the nineteenth century.

[24] *Cf.* Sturzo, p. 122.

[25] Sforza, pp. 332–334 and 311–312, he quotes the Irish Catholic, D. A. Binchy, in *Church and State in Fascist Italy*, to the same effect; Sturzo, pp. 123–124.

pacifist; the new conservative, Fascist, archnationalist, chauvinist, cynical opportunist.

A protracted courtship, no less publicly ardent for the distaste Mussolini privately displayed, led up to the *mariage de convenance* between fascism and Catholicism that was solemnized in the Lateran Pacts of 1929.

Mussolini's father named him for Benito Juárez, that stout Mexican foe of churchly privilege, and from his earliest years instilled anticlericalism in him. It stayed with him all his life. As a Socialist journalist, he had bitterly denounced the clergy; as a Fascist candidate for the Chamber of Deputies (1919), he had urged the confiscation of episcopal properties. His opportunistic alliance with the Church always rankled: three months after signing the 1929 concordat, the Duce burst out in the Chamber of Deputies that in Fascist Italy the Church was neither sovereign nor free. Had Christianity remained in Palestine, he said, it would have died there, "leaving no trace"; it was Rome that made it catholic;[26] the Lateran agreements had not "resurrected the temporal power of the popes": they "merely left [the papacy] enough territory to bury its corpse."[27] The Duce let Fascist hierarchs criticize the Church with impunity, Fascist "intellectuals" parade their Nietzschean and Sorelian anticlerical inspiration: if he generally concealed his own anticlericalism from the public, he kept it no secret from his associates.[28]

But Mussolini had read Machiavelli (and Plato) : he knew that "ecclesiastical principalities . . . are sustained by ancient religious customs . . . [that] keep their princes in power in whatever manner they proceed and live"; he understood full well how greatly clerical support would facilitate his totalitarian state. Long before the March on Rome, he had resolved to hitch the Church to his chariot.

[26] Speech of May 13, 1929: in a letter to Cardinal Gasparri May 30, the pope called this "heretical, and worse than heretical." See Jemolo, p. 639 ff.; Sforza, pp. 341–342.

[27] As reported in newspapers of May 14, 1929, the official text read, "We have buried it [temporalism]". See Jemolo, p. 641.

[28] Count Galeazzo Ciano, *The Ciano Diaries* (Garden City, N.Y., 1946) , pp. 25–26, 226, 229, 318, 423–425, 451–452.

As early as 1921, Mussolini had extolled to the Chamber the papacy's world importance and declared it Italy's duty to end the old dispute so as to use their "moral force" for her benefit. The day of Pope Ratti's election, the future Duce cast an eye over the hundreds of thousands assembled to acclaim the new pontiff, and observed thoughtfully:

"Look at this multitude of every country! How is it that the politicians who govern the nations do not realize the immense value of this international force, of this universal spiritual Power?"[29]

Soon after the weak-willed Facta government resigned before his blackshirts' threats and the equally weak-willed Victor Emmanuel made him prime minister, Mussolini launched his campaign to win over the Church.[30]

Cardinals, bishops, priests sore from the pinpricks of Garibaldian anticlericalism now found themselves courted, flattered, honored. Again, as in the good old days, no public ceremony was held without bishop or priest there to bless it. Clerics found themselves once more influential: their recommendation carried as much weight as politicians' in the Rome ministries and prefectures.

One of the Mussolini government's first acts was to present to the Vatican the valuable Chigi library obtained with the government's purchase of that midtown palace in 1918. Mussolini had installed his Foreign Ministry there: bureaucrats quipped that the Duce's big ideas required room, so the books had to go. But the gesture was exquisitely calculated to please the bibliophile who sat on Peter's throne.

A few days later, the Fascists announced early restoration of compulsory religious (Catholic) instruction in primary schools; shortly, Church schools were given full parity with public ones; there was talk of government aid to Italian schools operated by religious congregations abroad. Anticlericalism was rooted out of universities: candidates for degrees learned that dissertations

[29] Teeling, *The Pope in Politics*, in Avro Manhattan, *The Catholic Church Against the Twentieth Century* (London, 1950), p. 108.
[30] The account of the Fascist courtship is largely based on Jemolo, p. 611ff.

critical of Church history or policy fared ill. And the Fascist government voted three million lire for war-damaged churches.

A distinctly Catholic color was, meanwhile, given the first Fascist youth organizations. Priests blessed their banners. They had their chaplains. Mass opened their quasi-military exercises.

And if persuasion failed, there were always the Fascist wrecker gangs. Communists and Socialists were their usual victims; but some Catholic critics had also felt the club, tasted the castor oil; so had priests (though the Vatican hushed up such inconvenient scandals) ; Catholic labor centers had been sacked. Were Pius diffident, shrines, churches, the Vatican itself might also suffer this methodical violence.

The Vatican—apparently believing it could "subdue the Devil with holy water"—responded eagerly to the Duce's overtures.

A ringing papal denunciation, in that still Catholic though anticlerical Italy of the early twenties, might well have destroyed fascism at the start (as Badoglio's troops could have dealt handily with the March on Rome had the king said the word) . But the pope's thunder was withheld.

Instead, Pius looked on benignly as the Popular (Catholic) party entered the Duce's first ministry and Popular deputies joined in the 306-to-116 vote of confidence that—despite Mussolini's ominous boast that he could have turned the "gray and dull" hall of the Chamber of Deputies into barracks—confirmed him in power. When some farsighted Populars, following Luigi Sturzo and Alcide de Gasperi, assailed "the pantheistic state and the deified nation,"[31] the pope subtly insinuated his disapproval and so destroyed the Catholic Party[32]—as later he did Christian Democracy elsewhere in Europe. And, one after another, Fascist hierarchs received evidence of his favor in high papal decorations.[33]

[31] At party convention in Turin, April, 1923: see Sturzo, p. 126.

[32] On this see, especially, Jemolo, p. 607ff. Sforza, Salvatorelli, Cilibrizzi, and every other Italian authority with pretensions to impartiality I have consulted agree: the Popular party's formal dissolution (with that of others) was accomplished by Mussolini's decree of Nov. 6, 1926; but he was flogging a dead horse.

[33] See Buonaiuti, p. 137.

Occasionally, Pius did speak, in guarded phrases, against Fascist violence.[34] Occasionally, he deplored the company the Duce kept, company that occupied high places in the party and government, especially when this gentry spouted publicly the anticlericalism Mussolini privately shared.[35] Fairly early in the Fascist rulē, he noted the trend to state-worship, and remarked critically upon it,[36] albeit in general terms unlikely to offend. For the Fascist regime, and for Mussolini himself, however, Pius had only tenderness: from the start, he equated the well-being of Church and nation with this "man of destiny"; Mussolini's near-miraculous escapes from assassination, he unhesitatingly attributed to Providence.[37]

But if the pope—who as head of the universal Church had to show some consideration for opinion abroad—mildly qualified his praise of the dictator, no such considerations restrained the Italian clergy. With few exceptions, cardinals, bishops, and priests closed their eyes to the fact that fascism was basically anti-Christian[38] and, almost as one man, sang its praises: "the language of the churches was often not very different from that of the House of the Fasces."[39]

This "era of good feeling" culminated in the Lateran Pacts of 1929.

Under the agreements signed at the Lateran Palace February 11, 1929,[40] the Holy See:

1. Declared the "Roman question" "definitely and irrevocably settled."

2. Renounced claim to Rome and the former papal states, accepted Italian unification, and recognized the House of Savoy as its ruling dynasty.

---

[34] For example, consistorial allocution of March 24, 1924.

[35] See Sforza, p. 339ff.

[36] His allocution of Dec. 20, 1926, just after Mussolini's proclamation of "everything and everyone for the state," declared the state made for man, not man for the state. In proclaiming the 1925 Holy Year, he had assailed political theories making "society or the state an end in itself. . . ."

[37] Allocutions of Dec. 24, 1925 and Dec. 20, 1926.

[38] See Jemolo, p. 597ff.

[39] Ibid., p. 667.

[40] Treaty, concordat, and financial protocol.

3. Agreed to keep out of politics, and forbade priests and religious to join political parties.

4. Promised to remain aloof from "all temporal disputes between nations" and from "international congresses convoked for the settlement of such disputes," unless contending parties appealed to it. (The Vatican kept the right to use "its moral and spiritual power" for peace.)

5. Accepted state approval of nominations to bishoprics and parochial benefices.

For its part, Fascist Italy:

1. Acknowledged the pope sovereign and independent in the tiny Vatican City State, and gave extraterritoriality to certain Church properties outside it.

2. Guaranteed the person of the pope to be as "sacred and inviolable" for Italy as the king's, and undertook to treat "offenses and injuries" of him, by word or deed, as *lèse majesté*.

3. Established Catholicism as the "sole religion of the state."

4. Extended religious instruction to secondary schools, this to be confided either to ecclesiastics or to lay teachers approved by diocesan officials.

5. Accepted clerical control of marriage, banned divorce, and gave Church courts jurisdiction in annulments (while leaving separations to civil courts).

6. Promised legal protection to the secrecy of the confessional.

7. Gave religious orders and associations full legal standing.

8. Debarred apostate and excommunicate priests from state jobs requiring their "immediate contact with the public."

9. Exempted clerics in major orders and religious in solemn vows from military training and combat duty, and ordinaries, rectors, and curates generally from noncombatant service as well.

10. Undertook to supplement revenues of some benefices.

11. Indemnified the pope for revenues lost with the 1870 occupation of the papal domains.[41]

---

[41] The amount was 1,750 million lire, at the then exchange rate $87,500,000. Many, including some Catholics, thought it too great: it was certainly more than Benedict proposed to ask. But, see Sturzo, p. 128.

12. Established diplomatic relations with the new Vatican State.

Who was the chief gainer from the accord?

By Pius XI's lights, the Church: she had in some measure turned the clock back to the good old days before 1848; she had re-established the symbol, if not the substance, of the popes' temporal sovereignty; with the ban on state employment of ousted heretics, she had regained civil support of the principle of the Inquisition and resharpened the blunted weapon of excommunication; above all, with the reinstitution of religious teaching in public schools (and the cohibiting of competing faiths implied in the establishment of Catholicism), she had (perhaps) improved chances that Italians would continue faithful to the Church.

Yet secular observers, almost unanimously, concluded that more advantages lay with Mussolini—as, two years later, Pius XI himself admitted.[42]

He had healed old wounds and solidified Italians behind him; he had won potent domestic endorsement of his regime and support of his policies; he had given fascism "great prestige in the Catholic world,"[43] just as with some non-Catholics his prestige began to wane; he had neutralized the last force in Italy able to challenge him effectively; above all, he had assured Catholicism as his stout ally when he embarked, as he shortly did, on the cynical imperialism that led straight to World War II.

The Duce's bitterest enemies doffed their hats to this stroke of genius.

How valuable to him the new ally was quickly became apparent.

The story of Mussolini's shoddy adventures of the thirties and early forties is too recent to require retelling here: the assault on Ethiopia, on the pretext of spurious frontier incidents and the plea of *Lebensraum,* and the subsequent knifing of the League of Nations; the dispatch of "volunteers" to help Franco, so as to

[42] In encyclical *Non abbiamo bisogno,* June 29, 1931.
[43] Herbert L. Matthews, *The Education of a Correspondent* (New York, 1946), p. 462.

"keep communism out of the Mediterranean"; the seizure of Albania; the treacherous attack on Greece; the stab in the back to France.

And the role of the popes, and the Italian clergy, and world Catholicism?

In the Ethiopian war: implicit papal agreement that Mussolini needed Ethiopia for expansion and defense,[44] hints to Haile Selassie to yield without fighting, publicly voiced hopes for realization of the needs of the "great and good" Italian people, share in Italy's "triumphal joy" at victory—nowhere, condemnation of this naked aggression; meanwhile, advocacy from virtually every Italian pulpit of (in Cardinal Schuster's phrase) the "Catholic Crusade," episcopal blessing of the banners of departing regiments, tirades in the Catholic press against the democracies and sanctions, enthusiastic clerical help—even contribution of votive offerings—in the collection of gold and silver (including, ironically, wedding rings) to finance the war; abroad, the powerful support of the Catholic hierarchy and laity, their opposition to sanctions.[45]

In the Spanish War: early papal recognition (1937) of Franco's nationalists (though the papal nuncio remained in Madrid to the war's end) ; unanimity of the high and the low Italian clergy in blessing the Duce's reluctant "volunteers" as "crusaders" against infidel Moscow; abroad, such blind Catholic ardor for Franco as to force predominantly Protestant states like the United States and England to betray the Republic.

In the seizure of Albania: papal rejection of British pleas for vigorous condemnation—in the interest of peace—of such brutal aggression; Pacelli, now reigning, merely deplored the flouting of "solemnly sanctioned" treaties, and lamented that the attack had taken place on Good Friday.[46]

The attacks on Greece and France: papal silence; fervent cler-

---

[44] But Jemolo notes, p. 668, that *L'Osservatore Romano* declared unacceptable the theory that need of "vital space" justified wars of conquest.

[45] Camille M. Cianfarra, *The Vatican and the War* (New York, 1945) , pp. 41–43; Jemolo, p. 668, *passim;* Michael de la Bedoyere, editor of British *Catholic Herald,* in Blanshard, *American Freedom,* p. 247.

[46] Easter homily, April 9, 1939.

ical efforts (this time, less successful) to fan patriotic support of the war.[47]

There was often, it is true, friction between the allies.

Fascist attacks on Catholic Action produced, June 29, 1931, Pius XI's famed encyclical *Non abbiamo bisogno* which, though held up to liberals abroad as an outright condemnation of Mussolini and fascism, was in fact chiefly defense of the lay arm of the papacy, of the Church's right to educate youth, and of Catholics' right to mental reservations in taking the Fascist oath to obey the Duce in all. A plea for concord closed the encyclical: peace was soon made; the Vatican meekly agreed to curb Catholic Action and put it under strict hierarchical supervision.[48]

There were also, from time to time, papal protests at fascism's neopagan training of Italian youth.[49]

In 1938, Mussolini's anti-Semitic laws, slavish emulation of Hitler's, stirred the aged pope to public wrath—but chiefly because their prohibition of mixed marriages challenged priestly control of matrimony.[50] (Still, Pius XI had in 1928 and again, shortly before the laws appeared, condemned anti-Semitism in general terms.)

Nevertheless, the record shows that Pius XI did not once publicly condemn Fascist totalitarianism on broad philosophical, humanitarian, Christian grounds: it was the deified state competing for the religious affections of the Catholic faithful, the usurper of asserted churchly prerogatives, the violator of the Lateran Pacts that he denounced.

Pius himself said:

". . . We have not desired to condemn the [Fascist] party

---

[47] Jemolo, p. 671.

[48] See Igino Giordani, ed., *Le Encicliche Sociali dei Papi da Pio IX a Pio XII (1864–1946)* (Rome, 1948), pp. 421-424. This encyclical contains the so-called defense of "freedom of conscience": it is defined as "the right of souls to obtain maximum spiritual good under the tutelage . . . of the Church."

[49] Ibid.; also, encyclical *Per la Azione Cattolica*, June 29, 1931, which assailed fascism's monopolizing of youth in the interest of an "ideology that avowedly resolves into a veritable pagan statolotry. . . ."

[50] Sforza, p. 342, notes that Pius XI, speaking in his last days to Milan nuns, called Mussolini's anti-Jewish laws "veritable apostasy."

and the regime as such. We have intended to point out and condemn that in their program and activity which we have viewed
. . . as contrary to Catholic doctrine and practice and hence irreconcilable with the name and the faith of Catholics. Thus we
believe that we have at the same time done the party itself and
the regime a good turn. . . ."[51]

It may well be that Pope Ratti finally repented of his pro-
Fascist policy. Count Sforza says he has "irrefutable documentary evidence which, unfortunately, cannot be published at present," that at the last the pope told old friends his "deepest grief"
was having compacted with "people without faith and without
God" like Mussolini and Hitler.[52] A story now often told is that
Pius XI begged his doctors to keep him alive long enough to let
him denounce to the Italian episcopate, on the tenth anniversary
of the Lateran agreements, the faithlessness of the dictators; he
died one day before that date;[53] the speech, if written, was—as
is custom—burned.

It was left to his successor, Pope Pacelli, to put the Church on
record against the *principle*, rather than the Duce's *practice*, of
totalitarianism.

By an accident of history, fascism first appeared in Italy:
blackshirts became prototypes for brownshirts, Heimwehr, Iron
Guard, Falange, all the other excrescences of the turbulent twenties and thirties.

Had the Church's friendliness for fascism in Italy been unique,
it could be dismissed as an aberration—the understandable, if la-
mentable, result of the coincidence of an old Italian inferiority
complex, an Italophile pope and Curia, political and economic
distress, panic fear of communism, Mussolini's convincing portrayal of the messiah. The error would still have been grave, if
only for its effects on Catholic popular belief in papal infallibili-
ty. But the damage would have been limited.

It must be recorded, however, that wherever fascism appeared
the Church was sympathetic, if not openly co-operative.[54]

[51] *Per la Azione Cattolica.*
[52] Sforza, p. 342.
[53] Ibid., p. 343.
[54] Sometimes cited as an exception is the papal denunciation of Charles

Dollfuss's "clerical-fascist" state in Austria—modeling its constitution after Pius XI's encyclical *Quadragesimo anno* (that ostensibly perpetuated the social teaching of Leo's *Rerum novarum*, but implicitly endorsed Mussolini's Corporative State) [55] —was dear to the Roman Curia. In Portugal the Jesuit-trained Salazar's ironically named *Estado Novo* (New State), also modeled after Mussolini's, from the outset received stout Catholic support; Salazar's achievement in imposing order by financial reforms (which made him the "indispensable man") outweighed the fact that he turned his little country into Western Europe's tightest police state. Only too well remembered is the hysterical Catholic support, in Italy and abroad, for the Spanish Fascists' assassination of the Republic. Only too recent are the Vatican honors lavished on Juan Perón (though not, be it said for the Pope's good taste, on Evita). And there was, of course, the brief, unhappy *mésalliance* with Hitler.

A paragraph or two only may be devoted to the matter of the Holy See's relations with Nazi Germany.[56]

To explain Pius XI's avidity for an agreement with Italian fascism, some Catholic writers theorize that he felt it required to contain a new "pagan, pantheistic State."[57] For Italy, this explanation is superfluous, if not tendentious. In the case of Germany, however, it is more tenable.

Maurras's *Action Française,* the politico-religious movement often called the forerunner of fascism. The Holy Office condemned some of Maurras's writings in 1914, but Pius X deemed publication of the decree inopportune; Pius XI finally published it in 1926; Mussolini jested that he "felt the wind of the bullet that hit Maurras." The question is too difficult for treatment here: it may only be said that there are important differences between Maurras's movement, which advocated monarchy as the only kind of French government compatible with Catholicism, and Italian fascism; the cases are not strictly comparable.

[55] Harold E. Fey, "Can Catholicism Win America?" *Christian Century,* Nov. 29, 1944–Jan. 17, 1945, charges that the American hierarchy's aim is to replace democracy with the corporative state; its inspiration, too, he says, is *Quadragesimo anno.*

[56] Heretofore unpublished documents on Vatican City-Berlin relations are to be found in . . . volumes of captured German papers published under the aegis of the State Department by the U.S. Government Printing Office.

[57] Binchy, in Sforza, p. 342.

The intelligent Mussolini rationalized fascism convincingly, for such wishful thinkers as Vatican prelates: Hitler's doctrine, patchwork of scraps from every ragbag, could be seen at once for the opportunistic mishmash it was. The Italian's cynical role as friend of the Church was well played, his anticlericalism concealed: the German early seized on Alfred Rosenberg's *Myth of the Twentieth Century,* that anti-Christian, anti-Semitic hodgepodge, as the Holy Writ of his neopagan creed; Strasser, Feder, Borman, others spouted hostility to Catholicism. Until 1938, when the anti-Semitic bug bit him lightly, Mussolini's ethnocentrism was merely the dim memory of Mazzini's Italian "mission": spurious "Aryanism" marked nazism from the start. Mussolini waited four years to enounce totalitarianism: Hitler waited one.

Thus it is quite likely true that, as Pius XII said after the war, the Vatican accepted the unexpectedly favorable concordat Hitler offered in 1933 in full knowledge of the sort of regime it was dealing with.

"Pacelli said he had worked to conclude the 1933 agreement in the hope that it would 'set up a formidable barrier to the spread of ideas at once subversive and violent' and that it would (as he said it in fact did) give German Catholics 'a juridical basis for their defense and a stronghold behind which to shield themselves in their opposition.'

"It was not, he added, 'that the Church had any illusions built on excessive optimism or that in concluding the concordat she had any intention of giving any form of approval to the teachings or tendencies of National Socialism.'[58]

Almost at once, the Nazis spat on the concordat. From an ally, the Church became overnight an enemy, an institution of Jewish origin. Catholic schools were closed, parish youth organizations dissolved, press, charities, unions suppressed, nuns and priests tried on morals and currency charges: prelates who protested were treated as political offenders. Secret orders to party

---

[58] Address to cardinals, June 2, 1945: this address, which defends at length Church policy in Germany, has for some reason failed to receive the attention it deserves. *Cf.* Charles Pichon, *The Vatican and Its Role in World Affairs* (New York, 1950) , p. 143.

members made it clear that the aim of national socialism, like that of Marxism, was utterly to destroy Christianity.

Pius XI protested privately, through diplomatic channels. But he bore the affronts in public silence until Passion Sunday of 1937, when he issued the encyclical *Mit brennender Sorge:* this denounced the Nazi doctrines that produced persecution of the Church, but not (as apologists contend) the totalitarian principle of German fascism. Thereafter, until Pius XI's death, Vatican and Wilhelmstrasse were at knives. When Hitler visited Mussolini, Pius XI ostentatiously went to Castel Gandolfo; he closed the Vatican Museum, which the Führer intended to visit.

As pope, Pacelli was at first conciliatory to Hitler.[59] But Cardinal Hlond's report of the Germans' "perverse sadism" in Poland, their murder of priests and mistreatment of Catholic prisoners, stiffened his back: though to the end he withheld denouncing Hitler, national socialism, or German aggression by name, he could say (as he did after the war) that he often contrasted "the demands and perennial laws of humanity and of Christian faith" with the "ruinous" Nazi preaching and practice.

It is difficult to determine the part Eugenio Pacelli—foremost papal diplomat of his time, executant of Pope Ratti's concordat policy, his secretary of state for eight vital years, evidently the man most likely to influence him—played in shaping Ratti's attitude toward Italo-German fascism.

A Catholic contention is that, as cardinal, Pacelli already considered it impossible "to reconcile the aims and methods of Fascist expansion with the basic policies of Pius XI and the fundamental principles of the Church itself," and that "this divergence continued to grow in both the moral and political spheres."[60] This hardly squares with the record.

In Munich, Pacelli had seen the red tide roll by. There and in Berlin, he had watched the progressive disintegration of Germany that ultimately produced Hitler. The Vatican's leading expert on Germany, he worked for the concordat with Nazi Germany.

[59] See Ciano, p. 47; Halecki, pp. 95-96; Reynolds and Eleanor Packard, *Balcony Empire* (New York, 1942) , p. 240.

[60] Halecki, p. 331.

In the Rome of 1931, as Mussolini prepared for open war over Catholic Action, the new secretary of state's personal diplomacy averted the breach;[61] significantly, part of the price of the Church paid for peace was the debarring from Catholic Action office of old Populars who had opposed fascism; it may have been in reward that Victor Emmanuel in 1932 gave Pacelli the Collar of the Order of the Annunziata. And some commentators would have it that several times in the thirties the cautious cardinal persuaded the impulsive old pope to tone down diatribes against the dictators' anti-Church measures.[62]

Just so, the opening months of Pacelli's pontificate tended to discredit the view that he had given up hope of coming to terms with the dictators.

As we have seen, the new Pope ascended the throne preoccupied over the threat of war, convinced that peace was of transcendent importance. Two courses were open to him: appeasement, or vigorous rallying of world Catholic opinion against aggression. Like Chamberlain and Daladier six months before, he chose appeasement: he muted Vatican criticism of Mussolini's and Hitler's anti-Church measures in the interest of his peace efforts. This policy, and an audience with Pacelli, persuaded Count Ciano that, "We [Fascists] can get along well with this Pope."[63] Mussolini—who had privately rejoiced at the death of the "obstinate old man" Ratti[64]—apparently thought likewise.

It was not long, however, before the Duce was as much at outs with Pacelli as he had been with Ratti.

By 1939, it had become apparent even to Mussolini (who, resenting mortality more bitterly than most mortals, grew testy with age) that the Italians' perfervid adoration of the early years had given place to weary resignation. His sacrifice of Austria, and his servile seconding of Hitler, were widely unpopular; his bellicose speeches grated: Ethiopia and Spain had been adventure enough: most Italians wanted peace, not war. Momentarily, the Duce temporized; nonbelligerence restored some of his pres-

[61] Jemolo, *op. cit.*, pp. 665–666.
[62] Cianfarra, *The Vatican and the War,* p. 79.
[63] Ciano, *Diaries,* p. 47.
[64] Cianfarra, *op. cit.*, p. 20.

tige. But he had not forsworn imperialistic expansion: he still meant war.

However, if he were to fire his reluctant people (whose war-like virtues he publicly praised but privately disparaged) to yet another "crusade," he needed expert help. Specifically, he needed the help of the Catholic clergy "to keep up military and civilian morale."[65] This was not 1931, when he could invite an open break with the Church in the reasonable certainty that many Italian Catholics would side with him. This was 1940, when an attack on the Church would coalesce the forces of Catholicism with the forces of peace. The situation gave Pope Pacelli much more freedom of action than Pope Ratti had.

Thus Mussolini could only fume, in his Palazzo Venezia *sanctum sanctorum*, as the "pacifist" Pope repeatedly urged peace, strove to keep Italy neutral, published Hlond's account of Nazi atrocities, telegraphed condolences to the rulers of the overrun Low Countries, received the hated Roosevelt's envoys, brought pressure on Pétain to prevent persecution of French Jews, and sheltered Italian refugees from fascism in the Vatican.

Yet all this, while it convinced some that Pacelli was "privately anti-Fascist," did not constitute formal denunciation of the dictatorships that, deliberately, had loosed upon humanity the Second World War: well into the closing years of the war an American journalist, after an audience with Pacelli that left him an impression of "discouragement and helplessness," lamented that "the most important religious figure in the world felt it was not desirable or possible to condemn in public an evil which he deplored in private."[66]

---

[65] Sturzo, *op. cit.*, p. 130.

[66] Matthews, *op. cit.*, pp. 485–486. In 1944, the Catholic Information Society of New York published a pamphlet, *Is the Pope Fascist?* It termed Pacelli "the only world leader before 1939 to speak out fearlessly and dogmatically against the twin evils of fascism and nazism," and adduced a number of quotations in substantiation. I have not seen the pamphlet, but Blanshard, *American Freedom*, pp. 240–241, declares that no quotation given is "specific, fearless or dogmatic in condemning the two primary doctrines of fascism, political dictatorship and the corporate state"; "the 'criticisms' of fascism are simply counterattacks upon Mussolini and Hitler for their encroachments upon the educational and political preserves of the Catholic Church."

My own examination of Pacelli's papers has not discovered one pronouncement in his first six years as pope that flatly condemns the principles of totalitarianism and dictatorship, or that holds up as sacred the individual freedoms they trample.

True enough, as secretary of state, Pacelli denounced Rosenberg's neopaganism, the "Nazi Nordic New Religion"; but this was merely echo of *Mit brennender Sorge.*

True enough, his first encyclical, *Summi Pontificatus,* remarked the deleterious effects of totalitarianism for peace:

"To consider the state as something ultimate to which everything else should be subordinated and directed, cannot fail to harm the true and lasting prosperity of nations. . . . The idea which credits the state with unlimited authority is not simply an error harmful to the internal life of nations, to their prosperity, and to the larger and well-ordered increase in their well-being, but likewise it injures the relations between peoples, for it breaks the unity of supranational society, robs the law of nations of its foundation and vigor, leads to violation of others' rights, and impedes agreement and peaceful intercourse."

This is all well; but it is highly theoretical, and so unlikely to impress men of action unfond of thinking in abstract terms: the encyclical notably omits mention of dictatorship, democratic principles, man's freedoms.

At what point along the trajectory of the Fascist dictatorships Pacelli's annoyance at their cavalier treatment of the Church became philosophical disapproval of their system is hard to say: here, as elsewhere, expedience and principle are probably intermingled. At all events, it was not until the allocution of Christmas Eve, 1945, with Mussolini and Hitler long dead in the smoldering ruins of their grandiose dreams, that Pacelli condemned totalitarianism in unmistakable terms. On that occasion, he said:

"The force of the totalitarian state! Cruel, heartrending irony! The whole surface of the globe reddened with the blood shed in these terrible years, cries aloud the tyranny of such a state.

"The fabric of peace would rest on a tottering and ever-threatening base, if an end were not put to such totalitarianism, which lowers man to the state of a mere pawn in the game of politics, a cipher in economic calculations. With a stroke of the pen it changes the frontiers of states; by a peremptory decision it deprives a people's economy—always part of its life as a nation—of its natural outlets; with ill-concealed cruelty it also drives millions of men, hundreds of thousands of families, in the most squalid misery, from their homes and lands, tears them out by the roots and wrenches them from a civilization and culture which they had striven for generations to develop. It also sets arbitrary bounds to the necessity and to the right of migration and to the desire to colonize. All this constitutes a policy contrary to the dignity and welfare of the human race. . . . Man in the framework of the family and of society . . . by his labor is lord of the world. Consequently this totalitarianism fails by what is the only measure of progress, namely the progressive creation of ever more ample and better conditions in public life to ensure that the family can evolve as an economic, juridic, moral, and religious unit."

This is satisfactory enough. So, too, are Pacelli's subsequent statements on the theme. It must be admitted, however, that they came very late in the day.

It may appear ingenuous, and evidence of an unduly sanguine temperament, if I here say that I have come to believe that, despite some appearances to the contrary, Pius XII today opposes totalitarianism out of principle rather than expedience.

But it appears to me that, almost uniquely, Pacelli has as pope gone on learning. I believe that the "old" Pope perceives—what the prelate and the cardinal and the "young" Pope did not—the inherent impossibility of compacting with totalitarianism (in however plausible form it appears), the irreconcilability of Christian and totalitarian philosophy. I believe that Pacelli's *de visu* examination of Fascist and Communist totalitarianism, and his consideration of the sorry fruits of appeasing it, have brought him intellectually (as well as politically) closer to Western (which is to say, today, American) democracy than any pope in history. I believe that, within the limitations of the respect traditionalism requires Pacelli to pay to his errant predecessors "of happy memory," he is attempting to found on his new sympathies the teaching of his church.

This belief about Pacelli's outlook is difficult of substantiation. I am myself somewhat suspicious of it: it may well be wishful thinking. Admittedly, it rests largely on intangibles, on personal impressions impossible to commit to paper, on personal esteem for the present Pope; and these are influences perilous to objectivity. Indeed, my view of Pacelli flies in the face of the whole history of the papacy. And—the objection most difficult to dismiss—the papal deeds, in some areas of Church influence, still all too often give the lie to the papal words.

If, however, my belief is correct, the shift of papal policy is revolutionary. It may have important effects for the future of Western civilization.

E. E. Y. Hales

Mussolini, Hitler, and Pius XI;

and

Communism, Peace, and Pius XII

The ensuing passages come from a history that bears the imprimatur of the late Francis Cardinal Spellman and was a selection of both the Thomas More Book Club and Catholic Book Club. The author, E. E. Y. Hales (1908–   ), received his M.A. degree at Oxford. He teaches history at Uppingham School and is Staff Inspector of History in the British Ministry of Education. Perhaps the best known of Hales's numerous books is a sympathetic study of Pope Pius IX (1846–1878), the unrelenting foe of nineteenth-century liberalism. In his discussion of Pius XI and the Italian and German dictators, Hales shows considerably more patience with the Vatican's attitude toward Fascism

SOURCE. From E. E. Y. Hales, *The Catholic Church in the Modern World: A Survey From the French Revolution to the Present*, pp. 261–280. Copyright © 1956 by Doubleday & Company, Inc. Reprinted by permission of Doubleday & Company, Inc., and Methuen & Co. Ltd.

than does Mr. McKnight. Does Hales exaggerate the danger of a
Communist takeover in Italy in the 1920s?

In the section dealing with Pius XII, only the paragraphs per-
taining to the war years are reprinted. How does Hales explain
the silence of Pius XII?

Mussolini, Hitler, and Pius XI

In each of the countries which participated in the First World
War, the peace saw a tendency towards reconciliation with the
Church. We have seen why this was so: the fellowship of the
trenches, and respect for the way the Catholics practiced their
faith; a religion which included pain and death within its central
mystery could no longer be so easily ignored.

In no country were these influences stronger than in Italy, for
no armies suffered greater hardships than did the Italian armies,
ill clad as they were for the ice and snow of the Alps or for the
festering heat of the plain of Lombardy, inadequately supplied
with arms, and called upon to contend with the better-equipped
Austrian and German armies possessed of a stronger military
tradition. Innately Catholic, in spite of all that had happened
since the days of Pio Nono, much of the young manhood of Italy
now became outwardly as well as inwardly reconciled to the
Church. Such men added greatly to the strength of the Christian
Democrats and of Catholic Action. Some of them were now organised by that remarkable Sicilian priest, Don Luigi Sturzo, into
a political party, the Popolari, a move made possible by the lift-
ing of the papal ban upon Catholic participation in Italian politics.
How strong was Catholic public opinion in Italy may be judged
from the fact that, only founded in January 1919, the Popolari
became in 1922 the most powerful party in the Italian Parliament. Their programme was partly religious and partly political.
They wanted to see freedom for religious orders and for the
schools, and a full return of Catholics into political life on every
front; they also wanted decentralisation of the administrative system, with effective power for the different provinces of Italy, and
proportional representation in the central Parliament.

But above all they were pacifists, their movement was a pro-test against the violence of all the different groups, from the ex-treme right to the extreme left, which were seeking to solve Ita-ly's postwar problems by violent action of one kind or another. For the postwar years were a time of bitter discontent in Italy. To the fearful suffering of the war itself had been added the dis-illusionment of a peace that gave the country much less than she felt she was entitled to; there was mass unemployment; and the parliamentary régime, to which the country was indifferent, showed no sign of possessing the power to meet the situation. Apart from the Popolari, only the violent elements were pos-sessed of any effective backing in the country; on the one hand the Syndicalists and Communists, with some of the more extreme Socialists; on the other, and opposed to them, the National-Syn-dicalists, organised by Edmondo Rossoni, and the Nationalists, or "Irredentists," whose pride was D'Annunzio—D'Annunzio, whose "mystique of blood" we have already met and who, after the war, became the hero of the hour because with his "legionar-ies," in Garibaldian fashion, he seized for Italy the port of Fiume denied to her by the diplomats at Versailles.

Whoever will look beneath the surface of the confused events of the postwar period in Italy will see not a straight fight between Communists (representing the workers) and Fascists (organised by the employers), which is an oversimplified picture drawn for purposes of propaganda; he will see rather a situation in which violent groups were striving for control, some of them looking to a nationalist or patriotic solution of the country's problems (as D'Annunzio did, or Rossoni's National-Syndicalists), others looking to an Anarchist or Communist solution, being opposed in principle to the Italian State as such. These latter, who should properly at this date still be called Syndicalists (though they were generally coming to be called Communists) were much the most numerous and powerful, and it was they who organised the violent seizure of the factories in October 1920, the event which most impressed itself upon the Italian imagination.

Mussolini, son of a Socialist blacksmith, and embracing the vi-olent syndicalism taught by Sorel, came to adopt, like Rossoni, a nationalist or patriotic solution to Italy's problems. But in 1920 he was still only the leader of a very small group of *Fasci di combattimento*. When, in January 1922, he allied himself with

Rossoni's group, he greatly strengthened his movement and gave it effective working-class support. Moreover, by that year some of the other claimants to power had been weakened. The Communist seizure of the factories had alarmed the country and had failed in its purpose. D'Annunzio had been driven out of Fiume by the Italian Government (which had secured legal international recognition of Italy's right to the port) and had lost some "caste" to Mussolini, who was becoming increasingly the favourite of the Nationalists and the Irredentists.

By October 1922 there were three effective groups in the country, Mussolini's Fascists, the Communists who looked to Moscow, and Don Sturzo's Popolari. All three were represented in Parliament, as were other parties. But a time had been reached when Italians were not looking to parliamentary political parties, as such, but to groups which had strong local support in the country. Disillusionment with the parliamentary parties, with the administration, and with the police, was so universal that it has been said, with some show of reason, that the issue in 1922 was not whether the parliamentary régime could withstand the outside groups, but which of the outside groups would fill the evident vacancy.

This is an exaggeration. What however can be said with confidence is that, when Mussolini's black shirts appeared outside Rome in October 1922 the King would not have been interpreting the popular will if he had used government troops to disperse them. The Fascists enjoyed the credit of having defeated the Communist offensive over the seizure of the factories, they enjoyed the credit of having lowered the red flags from public buildings all over Italy, of having reversed a situation in which the veterans of the World War were made to feel ashamed of having fought for Italy. The government of the premier, Facta, enjoyed no credit at all. If the troops had been turned against the Fascists it would have been the signal for civil war, and the most likely result would have been a Communist victory.

Don Sturzo, leader of the Popolari, later blamed himself for negotiating with the other political parties during the critical year 1922 and not boldly himself taking office. But it must remain doubtful whether it was really possible for him to do so. In southern Italy, certainly, the Popolari were supreme. But a party which was avowedly pacifist, which "turned the other cheek" when its buildings and property were attacked by the Communists or the Fascists, could hardly have taken over the government of the country at this juncture, when not only the Communists and the Fascists, but the still strong anti-clerical Liberals and Socialists, of different shades, were all opposed to it. Moreover the Popolari only enjoyed the qualified approval of the hierarchy and of the papacy. We have seen how anxious Leo XIII and Pius X had both been to ensure that Christian Democracy was properly under episcopal control. We have seen how one of its leaders, Murri, had become an advanced Modernist. Sturzo had avoided that heresy; but he and his movement were widely regarded as "demagogic," and even as a "white bolshevism," to be compared with the "red bolshevism" of the Communists. These doubts on the part of the hierarchy may indeed have served to help the Popolari in the country, by placing them in the position of the German Centre party and demonstrating that they were free from "priestly control," that they were a non-clerical Catholic party. But they did not help to put Don Sturzo into power, because for that the support of the King (who regarded him as a dangerous radical) and in some measure of the hierarchy also would have been needed.

Rightly or wrongly—and we must allow at least that the decision was understandable—the King decided that the choice really lay between Mussolini and the Communists, and he chose the former. It was not a choice which could be palatable to the new Pope Pius XI, since Mussolini was an avowed atheist and boasted of it; moreover his Fascists, when not fighting the Communists, were often enough to be found attacking the houses of the Christian Democrats or breaking up the meetings of the Popolari. Yet the Pope, like Victor Emmanuel III, was confronted with a choice of evils, and no greater evil than a Communist victory could present itself. Mussolini was preferred as the lesser danger. When, in the following year (1923), having got the Communists under control, the Fascists turned their attention more seriously to crushing the Popolari, a dangerous situation arose in which an all-out Fascist assault upon the Church was threatened. To avert this danger Don Sturzo resigned the leadership of the party and the challenge of the Popolari was over.

Christian Democracy, as a political force, gradually disappeared from the scene until after the Second World War.

In the sense described, but only in that sense, it may be said that Rome connived at the Fascist victory. It is hard to see what alternative she had, but easy to see how she suffered at the hands of the new dictator. Mussolini was not, as Napoleon had been, a Catholic by early upbringing. The piety of his mother had been overborne by the scorn of his Socialist father. But like Napoleon he was a realist; finding himself ruling over a country still predominantly Catholic, he would try to reach an accommodation with the Church.

What made that accommodation well-nigh impossible was a clear conflict of ideology, which involved a clear conflict over education. Mussolini's régime, like Napoleon's, depended upon his securing control over the minds and spirits of Italians and winning from them a devotion which can only rightly be called religious. Fascism, however pagan, was certainly religious in character, because it demanded devotion, self-sacrifice, and complete self-surrender to the nation, the party, and the Duce. Mussolini himself defined it, in the Italian Encyclopaedia, as a "conception of the State, its character, its duty, and its aim. Fascism conceives of the State as an absolute, in comparison with which all individuals or groups are relative, only to be conceived of in their relation to the State . . ."

How were Italian boys, very many of whom had been notably indifferent about the new State, to be made to feel in this way about it? By "moral teaching" in the state schools; by "doctored" Italian history; by entry, at the age of six, into the *Figli della lupa* (children of the wolf, the wolf which suckled Romulus and Remus) ; by proceeding to the *Balilla,* the *Avanguardia,* and, at the age of eighteen, to the *Giovani Fascisti*; by becoming at twenty-one, if they were found worthy, full-fledged members of the Fascist party proper.

Against this scheme of indoctrination Pius XI waged a ceaseless warfare. The foundation of it, the notion that, in comparison with the State, all individuals or groups had only a relative significance, he castigated as a monstrous inversion, a denial of the primary rights of the individual, the family, the Church, all of

which came before the State, whose business it was to protect
them. As against the state monopoly of education, which allowed
only a brief period of religious instruction to the Church, he
claimed her right to run schools. As against the para-military
youth clubs of Fascism he defended the cause of the Catholic
clubs; especially dear to him were the Catholic boy scouts, whom
he was compelled to dissolve in 1927. Even more important to
the Church was Catholic Action, a world-wide movement
launched by Pius XI and intended to enlist Catholic laymen
effectively in societies for their mutual spiritual benefit, and that
they might the better influence public life in a Catholic direction.
Mussolini compelled the Pope in 1931 severely to curtail the
scope of Catholic Action's activities in Italy, excluding it from
politics and from the corporations and syndicates which had replaced the trade unions. We have seen . . . how the economic
structure of the Fascist Corporate State was criticised by the
Pope for tending to "substitute itself in the place of private initiative instead of limiting itself to necessary and sufficient assistance." This was in Pius XI's encyclical *Quadragesimo Anno*, of
1931, which reiterated, in the face of the Fascists, the principles
of *Rerum Novarum*. But much more striking was his encyclical
Non Abbiamo Bisogno, of the following month (June 1931),
which he had to smuggle out of Rome and publish in France. In
it he denounced the "brutalities and beatings, blows and blood-
shed," the monopoly of youth "from tenderest years up to manhood and womanhood, for the exclusive advantage of a party
and of a régime based on an ideology which clearly amounts to a
real pagan worship of the State—Statolatry—which is no less in
conflict with the natural rights of the family than it is in contradiction with the supernatural rights of the Church." In this encyclical Pius XI specifically declared that the oath of blind obedience required by the régime from the members of its youth
organizations was "unlawful."

In the face of so violent an antagonism the measure of support
which Mussolini certainly did, from time to time, receive from
Pius XI may seem surprising. The two rulers shared, however,
certain common objectives and certain common qualities. First
and most important was the antagonism they felt towards com-

munism, and their determination that it should not capture Italy. The victory of Lenin in Russia, and after him of Stalin, had given an edge to the teachings of Marx and Bakunin, which the Russian dictators amplified and expounded in new treatises which only underlined the materialist basis of the Communist philosophy of life, and the "necessity of atheism," while the whole Western world was being shocked by the Russian anti-God campaign, with its ridicule of crucifixes and other holy symbols. When Pius XI and Mussolini both came to power in 1922 it was only a matter of months since not only Italy but Austria, Hungary, and even Germany had seemed likely to fall to communism; it was only natural that the Pope should have some sympathy, at first, for a régime which seemed likely to save Italy from such a fate.

The Pope and the dictator also shared a certain quality of political realism, which made it possible for them to do business together. Pius knew that the sixty years' quarrel with the Italian State was a grave source of weakness to the Church in Italy; Mussolini knew that the same quarrel was a grave source of weakness to the State. Whereas previous Popes had been impressed by the brutality of the new State's anti-clerical policies, and had supposed that its extreme political instability meant that it was unlikely to survive, the outcome of the First World War had shown that the Italian nation was a reality, however weak, and, from the Church's point of view, a reality preferable to either the anarchy or the communism which seemed to be the only alternatives in the peninsula. It was time to end an anomalous state of things and, after two years of secret and hard bargaining between Cardinal Gasparri (Pius' Secretary of State) and Mussolini's government, the Lateran Treaty of February 1929 created an independent and sovereign Vatican State and endowed it with some two billion lire—a smaller sum than the accumulated annual payments due to the papacy under the old Law of Guarantees of 1871 (and untouched by the Pope) but useful to meet the expenses of refitting the Vatican and building new administrative offices. To the Pope the important point was that he should be independent and sovereign; it did not matter how small his state was—indeed the smaller the better.

To the treaty was closely tied a concordat with Italy to govern the status of the Church in the country. Catholicism became once more the official religion to be taught in the schools. Catholic marriage became once more legal and sufficient; it was no longer necessary for there to be a civil ceremony as well. The status of the religious orders was safeguarded. Catholic processions were now protected, and the proselytising activities of Protestant bodies (but not of course their freedom of worship) were restricted. Nevertheless, as we have already seen, deep-seated causes of conflict remained, centering around Catholic Action and the Catholic schools. The Pope was not prepared to regard the doctrinal instruction given in the state schools as the limit of the Church's legitimate educational activities. Mussolini was not prepared to allow Catholic Action (protected by the Concordat) to have any political scope. And he required the liquidation of the Catholic boy scouts and girl guides in favour of his own militaristic organisations.

All the same, the treaty and Concordat were sensible measures which strengthened the hold of the Church upon Italy, and if the spectacle, so widely published in the press, of the Duce kneeling in front of the Apostle's statue in St. Peter's was rightly received with more reserve than Napoleon's coronation in Notre Dame had enjoyed, it yet served a similar purpose.

Until his death in 1939 Pius XI continued to find Mussolini and his régime a dangerous ally, and one he was constantly driven to criticise and even to denounce; he is reported on one occasion to have likened dealing with Mussolini to dealing with the devil. Yet an ally on the whole he remained, because on the whole Mussolini's enemies were also the enemies of the Church. Such, for instance, were the Freemasons, who had been for a century and more the most implacable enemies of the Church in Italy, and who now found the activities of their lodges, their banks, and their press curtailed by the Fascist régime. Such, across the Mediterranean, was the Coptic Church in Northeast Africa, which Mussolini indirectly helped to expose to Catholic influences, as a result of his encouragement of emigration, and of his conquest of Ethiopia in 1935.

But it was in Spain that the interests of the Church and of the Italian State most nearly coincided.

We have seen already . . . the pass to which matters had come for the Church in Spain by the year 1936. It was not so much a matter of anti-clerical legislation of the customary kind, intended to secularise the life of the country—though the Republic had gone further in this direction than any previous Spanish régime. It was rather the violence of Anarchist and Communist mobs, especially in Catalonia, which led to the burning of churches on a scale not previously seen save in Mexico. The winning of power by a left-wing government with Anarchist elements in 1936 aggravated the situation, because the power of the State no longer stood in defence of the Church. When the civil war started, in July 1936, it was inevitable that the Church, in self-defence, should side with the Nationalist movement in support of General Franco. In their collective letter of the following July the Spanish bishops explained to their brethren throughout the world why the Church "in spite of its spirit of peace, and in spite of not having wanted the war nor having collaborated in it, could not be indifferent to the struggle." As the struggle went on, the extremists on both sides necessarily grew stronger, and outrages were not confined to either. Neutrality, for Spaniards, became an impossibility. For the Church it was a simple issue of survival. By the year 1938, in Barcelona, which had become the republican capital, it had ceased to be a matter of isolated mob attacks upon convents or churches. It was the Paris of 1793 once again—only the bishop's chapel was tolerated, the churches were closed, priests had to disguise themselves, and Mass had to be said in secret. Already in March 1937, in *Divini Redemptoris,* Pius XI had recorded: "Not only this or that church or isolated monastery has been sacked, but as far as possible every church and every monastery has been destroyed. Every vestige of the Christian religion has been eradicated, even though intimately linked with the rarest monuments of art and science! The fury of Communism has not confined itself to the indiscriminate slaughter of bishops or of thousands of priests and religious of both sexes; it searches out above all those who have been devoting their lives to the working classes and the poor. But the majority of its victims have been laymen of all conditions and classes. Even up to the present moment masses of them are slain almost daily for no other offence than the fact that they are good Christians or at least opposed to atheistic Communism. And this fearful destruction has been carried out with a hatred and a savage barbarity one could not believe possible in our age."

Mussolini, on the other hand, was interested in the Spanish struggle for reasons of power politics as well as of ideology. The Popular Front Republican government in Madrid was unwelcome to him because it orientated Spain politically towards the Popular Front government in Paris, whereas previously the Spanish Government of Primo de Rivera[1] had looked rather towards Rome. A friendly Spanish Government, which might provide him with submarine bases in the Balearic Islands, or on the east coast of Spain, was an important factor to him in his attempt to rival French and British naval power in the Mediterranean. But ideology probably mattered to him more. A left-wing government at Madrid, with Anarchist and Communist elements, at the same time as a Popular Front government in Paris, was a serious challenge to the ideology upon which his own régime rested, and it became more serious when Moscow interested herself in maintaining it there.

On the ideological side, then, the Pope's and Duce's views about Spain had much in common: both feared the Communists. But they did so for different reasons. Mussolini had little concern for the Church. Pius had little for Fascism—how little may be judged by his devastating encyclical, *Mit Brennender Sorge,* of March 1937 (the same month as his *Divini Redemptoris* on Communism), in which he assailed the Hitler régime in Germany.

It is of course inaccurate to use the word fascism, which properly belongs to the Italian movement, for Hitler's Nazi régime. But by the year 1937, which we have now reached, the two movements had in fact grown closer together; for the Berlin-Rome Axis had become a working reality in Spain, and the two dictators were bringing their régimes into harmony—which meant that Mussolini was being compelled to adopt attitudes dictated by his more powerful partner. If a régime already brutal could properly be described as being brutalised, one would so

[1] General Miguel Primo de Rivera was military dictator of Spain from 1923 to 1930. His son, José Antonio, founded the fascistic Falange Español in 1933. *Ed.*

describe the effect of nazism upon fascism. Amongst the early consequences of the new alliance was the persecution, for the first time, of the Jews in Italy. And another was a renewed hostility between Church and State—a hostility demanded by Hitler. For it was intolerable to the German dictator that his colleague across the Alps should be on friendly terms with the author of *Mit Brennender Sorge*.

Hitler had been brought to power in Germany in 1933 by circumstances analogous with those which had brought Mussolini to power eleven years earlier in Italy; but the analogy should not be pressed too far. At elections which were still free he had won, in 1932, 230 seats in the Reichstag, or more than a third of the total, which was a far larger parliamentary following than Mussolini won before he seized power at Rome. True, this figure dropped to 190 at the next election, in November of the same year but, by allying with von Papen and the Nationalists, Hitler manoeuvred himself constitutionally into power in January 1933, and only in the subsequent election (March 1933) was he in a position effectively to influence the outcome by terror tactics. The previous four years had been a period of growing crisis in Germany, caused by the great depression, the mounting unemployment, and the rioting of the "Reds," whose gains in the Reichstag had been only a little less spectacular than those of the Nazis. Dissatisfaction with parliamentary government, as it had been practised by the Weimar Republic (the postwar successor of Imperial Germany) was being felt both on the right and on the left; the call, as always on such occasions, was for a "strong hand." To obtain full emergency executive powers under the constitution it was necessary for Hitler to secure a two-thirds majority in the Reichstag; even after the elections of March 1933 he could only obtain such a majority with the support of the Catholic Centre party. The responsibility, then, of the Centre (representing a large proportion of German Catholicism) for the tragedy that was to follow was that, by voting these powers to Hitler, it enabled his dictatorship to begin.

In the light of what followed that is a very grave responsibility. But it did not seem so at the time. A Reichstag in which the strongest parties were the Nazis, on the one hand, and the Socialists and Communists on the other, was not a body which seemed likely to provide an executive capable of governing quietly in a parliamentary manner. As elsewhere in Europe the choice seemed to rest between the Right and the "Reds," and if President von Hindenburg, the Grand Old Man of Germany, was prepared to swallow his social prejudices and call Hitler to power, that seemed to many a sufficient guarantee that he was indispensable to the maintenance of law and order.

Such was the line of thought of respectable small men of the middle class, the "backbone of Germany," men who had always given their support to the Centre party, men who believed in the family, in order, in hard work, and who feared the Communists as the sworn foes both of Catholicism and of the whole social order. Hitler stood for Germany, for discipline, for effort—and against the "Reds." That was enough for them—and, it should be added, for most of the German hierarchy too. And some of the more thoughtful Catholics were reassured by von Papen. Here was a man who was a zealous Catholic, of good family, who was willing to work with Hitler, who had made him vice-chancellor; von Papen, they believed, would "civilise" the new chancellor and keep him on the rails.

That he would need some civilising could not be denied because was he not, after all, the author of *Mein Kampf*, that notably un-Catholic book, and had not the bishops, earlier on, felt obliged to excommunicate the leading members of his party? But the general attitude in 1933 was that power (especially with Hindenburg above him and von Papen at his side) would make Hitler responsible, that *Mein Kampf* was a youthful indiscretion, to be taken no more seriously now than were the young Mussolini's atheistic diatribes as a revolutionary hothead in Switzerland. The excommunication was lifted in the same month as the full powers were voted, and von Papen proceeded forthwith to negotiate a concordat with Rome, which was completed with remarkable rapidity and signed in July of the same year. Cardinal Gasparri, who had negotiated the Lateran Treaty and Concordat with Mussolini in 1929, had been succeeded as Pius XI's Secretary of State by Cardinal Eugenio Pacelli (the future Pope Pius XII) and to him belongs much of the credit for completing the new concordat. Ever since 1920, as nuncio first at Munich and then at Berlin, Pacelli had striven to secure a concordat with the Weimar Republic; but he had only succeeded in securing separate concordats with the governments of Bavaria and Prussia. The new concordat with Hitler's Germany, so rapidly concluded, seemed a happy augury. It secured freedom for the Church in Germany to administer its own affairs, the State retaining the right of veto over episcopal appointments and requiring an oath of loyalty to the Führer. There was to be freedom of communications with Rome, freedom for the religious orders, permission to establish Catholic theological faculties at the universities, and Catholic public primary education.

On paper it was a good concordat, and Rome is not in the habit of refusing the opportunity of negotiating such instruments for the protection and regulating of the life of the Church. And although the papal Secretary of State already knew only too much about Hitler, he had also to consider that the Catholic vice-chancellor, von Papen, was pressing the negotiations, that Hindenburg was still Head of the State, and that the Centre party had given its support to the new government. He had reason to hope that the concordat might serve to strengthen the sane and moderate men who stood around the new chancellor. And if Hitler had no intention of abiding by it, why had he asked for it?

For Hitler the concordat had a certain prestige value. In a matter of months he had brought to a successful conclusion negotiations which had eluded the Weimar Republic for more than ten years. Moreover a gesture of friendship towards the Centre party was opportune. He needed its support in those early months. Nor did he seriously assail the Church until after the vote of the Catholic people of the Saar, in the plebiscite of 1935, had safely landed that territory in the German net. But the Centre party proved to have been deluded when it supposed that the new régime might be civilised. It was not the only group which suffered from that delusion, which was shared by sober senators of the United States and by cautious conservatives in England. The fact was that nobody quite believed that any government, once in power, could really attempt to carry out the programme of *Mein Kampf*.

Within five days of the signature of the concordat Hitler showed how irreconcilable were his racial theories with Catholicism when he promulgated a law for the compulsory sterilisation of certain classes of the community. In the following year he called to power the fanatical philosopher of Aryanism, Alfred Rosenberg, whose *Myth of the Twentieth Century* Rome placed on the Index. The government replied by suppressing the pastoral letter in which the German bishops refuted Rosenberg's theories. Meanwhile the persecution of the Jews had begun, Cardinal Faulhaber, at Munich, was defending those "ancestors of all Christians according to the spirit," in his famous sermons, and soon brave bishops, such as the heroic Cardinal Galen of Münster, or Preysing of Berlin, were condemning not only the laws which forbade intermarriage between Aryans and Jews, but the whole horrid heresy.

Although there were not lacking those who continued to suppose that, by its emphasis on work, order, discipline, obedience, sacrifice, and the like, nazism could provide a temporal habitude for Catholicism, the truth was that, as Hitler came to give more scope to Rosenberg and Goebbels, so his *mystique,* in its more revolting elements of race, blood, and conquest, became more apparent, and the more moderate men with whom he had surrounded himself at the start disappeared into the background or right off the stage. By the year 1937, although German arms, alongside Mussolini's, were helping to withstand the Communists in Spain, Pius XI issued *Mit Brennender Sorge* in condemnation of nazism. Printed secretly in Germany, it was read from the pulpits and it constituted, in the eyes of Germans and in the eyes of the world, the most serious public denunciation of Hitler's régime and its ideals to which the dictator was ever subjected in Germany. The Pope spoke of "the vain attempt to imprison God, Creator of the Universe . . . within the confines of a common blood or a single race," of "aggressive neo-paganism," of a "war of extermination" waged against the Church. Hitler replied, in November 1937, by saying that "recognition of the importance of blood and of race raises itself today above a humanist conception of the world . . . it is a victorious idea which is spreading like a wave across the entire world."[2]

---

[2] Extracts from Hitler's speech are printed in J. Rovan, *Le Catholicisme politique en Allemagne* (Paris, 1956), p. 237.

So much for the conflict on the absolute plain of beliefs. On the practical plain of action it demonstrated itself in attacks upon Catholic Action, in all its branches, and especially in its youth clubs, which were not to be allowed to compete with the Hitler Youth; in violation of the concordat in respect of Catholic education and the freedom of the religious orders; in flagrant interference with liberty of speech, the press, and communications with Rome. Yet it was not until the Second World War had actually broken out that Hitler could be said to have waged a Kulturkampf. Wholesale imprisonment and execution of priests did not begin till then, and there still remained those who thought that an accommodation was possible. Such were von Papen, who had become ambassador at Vienna, and, amongst the Austrians with whom he was in contact, Cardinal Innitzer and the Chancellor Schuschnigg. The *Anschluss*, by which Hitler in March 1938 swallowed up Austria, was applauded by Cardinal Innitzer, whose indecent haste in recommending the new régime to the faithful earned him the rebuke of Rome. The anti-Catholic campaign which followed the *Anschluss* in Austria was directed primarily towards converting the Austrians from Catholicism to Nazi beliefs; for this reason it was directed against Catholic education, from the primary schools up to the universities.

A distinction may be noted here between the Nazi campaign and that of Bismarck. Whereas the latter had believed in the value of the Church and was concerned to gain control over it, so as to make sure that it gave support to his régime, Hitler's personal standpoint was fundamentally antithetical to Christianity as such. If he spared the churches and allowed the Mass to continue to be said, thereby deceiving many Catholics as to his real intentions, it was only because he felt he could not yet afford their outright opposition.

With the outbreak of the Second World War the pace of persecution quickened. The Catholic schools were closed and the Catholic press was suppressed. In the rapidly overrun territories of Poland (almost wholly Catholic) convents, monasteries, and seminaries were closed and their occupants, together with hundreds of the secular clergy, were sent to the notorious concentration camp at Dachau. By March 1945 there were 1493 priests, from all over the Reich, at Dachau alone.[3]

It is small wonder that when the one serious attempt to get rid of Hitler was organised, in July 1944, some of the leaders amongst the conspirators were Catholics and the chief amongst them, Colonel von Stauffenberg, fervent in the Faith. And with them stood Lutheran and other Protestant leaders. Informed Christian leaders knew by then what has since been brought to light by the Nuremberg trials, namely that the proscription of the Churches, required by Nazi ideology, was to be pursued after victory with the aid of "evidence" of the unpatriotic activity of priests, which the Gestapo was already collecting.

Potentially the Nazi threat to the Church was as serious as any it had encountered; but just as that had not been apparent in 1933 so, even during the Second World War, the full rigours of persecution were not released save in Poland, the Poles being treated as an inferior, subject people, and their religion as requiring no respect. In France, Belgium, and Holland, where the Nazi aim was to enlist co-operation, priests as such were not proscribed, while in Germany, although very many were sent to concentration camps, we do not find the archbishops and bishops generally imprisoned, as many were by Bismarck, though we need not doubt that their turn would have come at the end of a successful war.

The result of these tactics was that many good Catholics, believing the constantly reiterated warning that their country was in danger, and that Hitler was an instrument sent for her salvation, to safeguard her from communism, saw it as their duty to give to his government the obedience to which all legitimate authority is entitled; and many of them died, alongside their fellows in the Russian snows, or in Siberian prison camps, without ever having understood the destiny which their Führer held in store for their Faith.

[3] Figures given by Rovan in *op. cit.*, p. 245.

Communism, Peace, and Pius XII

The end of the Second World War brought with it major changes in the political balance of the world. The United States of America and the Soviet Union emerged as the two strongest powers, with Great Britain a rather uneasy third. Eastern Europe, as far as Berlin, Vienna, and Constantinople, fell under the control of Moscow, while the victory of the Communists in China brought the most populous country in Asia under a Communist government, and into friendly relations with the Soviet Union. Since the land forces of Russia were incomparably stronger than those of any other power, an ominous challenge to Europe and to Asia was set up at a time when the strongest traditional armies on the two continents, those of Germany and Japan, had gone down to total defeat.

From the point of view of Britain, France, and the other governments of western Europe, the situation was made much more serious by the fact that Communist parties emerged in the West, and notably in Italy and France, large enough to constitute the principal opposition parties in those countries, and even likely, in Italy at least, to win political power. It was a very much more serious situation than had arisen after the First World War. Moreover these parties were backed by the might of Russian arms, now thrust right into the centre of Europe.

The danger implicit in allowing such a situation to develop had been more evident to the British war leader, Winston Churchill, than to the American President, Franklin Roosevelt. It is no part of the purposes of this book to enter into the controversies, which will not for long be resolved, concerning the "bargain" struck between Roosevelt and Stalin at Yalta in 1944,[4] or concerning Churchill's dislike of the plan to invade southern France, in preference to an invasion of the Balkans, though it is relevant to notice here that a successful Balkan invasion might

[4] *Sic*. The Yalta Conference of the Big Three lasted from February 4–11, 1945. *Ed*.

well have had an important effect, after the war, upon the position of the Russians in eastern Europe. What we need to consider is the important fact that eastern Europe was "liberated" by the Russian armies, which made little use of local resistance movements. The heroic Polish uprising, for example, at Warsaw, was left isolated to be crushed by the Nazis, although the Russian armies were on the doorstep in overwhelming strength. The leadership in occupied eastern Europe was to be Russian leadership, a military control responsible to Moscow. It goes without saying that this was not what the Wetern powers wanted but they were compelled, in 1945 at Potsdam, to accept it.

If Churchill had harboured few illusions about Soviet intentions, it was even more certain that Pope Pius XII had harboured none at all. Although he had eschewed any criticism of Stalin or his régime whilst Russia had been fighting for her life, he knew much better than Roosevelt that the Communist aim was a Communist Europe, controlled from Moscow, and that the Soviet Government would not voluntarily stop the advance. And he knew, too, what this would mean for religion.

As Secretary of State since 1930, the future Pope had been the right hand of Pius XI, a ruler who had understood where the greatest danger lay, and who had consistently denounced the persecution of religion in Russia, in Spain, or in Mexico, and had exposed the menace implicit in Communist and "fellow-travelling" teaching. Despite his robust attacks upon the Nazi ideology, and his indignation at Fascist statolatry, Pius XI, together with his Secretary of State, had never lost sight of the fact that, as Chief Shepherd of the Church, the Pope must keep his eyes upon the main menace to the flock, and already Pope and Secretary could see clearly enough where this was to be found.

But as the danger of war, in 1938 and 1939, had grown greater, they were also bound to strive, by all the means at their disposal, to preserve peace. This was Pius XII's first preoccupation, in that fateful first year of his pontificate, which was the year 1939. Those who wanted to see him denounce the régimes of Hitler and Mussolini more openly and more immediately than his predecessor forgot that his overriding aim was, by avoiding openly taking sides between the Western powers, to reach a position from which he might hope to be able to help to negotiate a just settlement between them. It would have been useless, as well as wrong, for him to take sides, in advance, on the international issues at stake between the Western powers, although he had gone so far in the previous summer, when still Secretary of State, as to administer a stinging rebuff to the two dictators, when they met in Rome, by withdrawing with the Pope to Castel Gandolfo.

Now, as Pope, in pursuit of peace, he endeavoured in May 1939, through his nuncios in Paris, London, Berlin, Rome and Warsaw, to promote a five-power conference to settle outstanding disputes about the Polish Corridor, and about the various points at issue between Italy and France. It was the only kind of initiative which could hope to relieve the crisis. But already the Vatican was becoming aware that serious negotiations were on foot between Hitler and Stalin, and these it was that precipitated the war and settled the fate of Poland. A last-minute appeal by the Pope, on July 30, having failed, there remained for the moment no more that the Vatican could do save to denounce the treatment of Poland, together with the coercion by Russia of the Baltic states, and to strive to avert a conflagration in the West. He concentrated chiefly, now, upon striving to keep Mussolini from joining in; in this endeavour he undoubtedly had the support of most of the Italian people. It was also an endeavour in which he had the valuable assistance of Roosevelt's personal representative at the Vatican, Myron Taylor, who arrived at the end of the same year.

In his Christmas message the Pope placed before the world, while the conflict was still confined to the East, his five-point plan for a peace. Avoiding specific territorial proposals, such as had been included in Benedict XV's proposals of 1917, he enunciated what he considered should be the principles of a general settlement: assurance to all nations, great or small, of their right to life and independence; delivery of the nations from the slavery imposed upon them by the armaments race; international institutions for maintaining peace; revision of treaties by peaceful methods; an appeal to all Christians, whether within the Catholic fold or without, to accept as their common ground the principles of justice and charity, under the Law of God, proclaimed in the Sermon on the Mount. A year later, in the London *Times,* the leaders of all the Churches in England specifically endorsed the Pope's principles—an unprecedented event.

The fall of Denmark, Norway, Holland, Belgium, and France to Hitler in the summer of 1940, and the entry of Mussolini into the war, brought to nothing the Pope's endeavours, and there was even some talk of his having to remove to Canada, as Rome became surrounded by belligerent forces; he determined, however, to remain. In June 1941 came Hitler's invasion of Russia and for three years, at least, in the overriding interests of peace, the Pope was silent about the Communist persecution of Christianity, since the Russian people very evidently were the victims of Hitler's aggression. But his forebearance was ill requited, for Moscow, with an eye upon the Catholics of eastern Europe, whom she intended to incorporate within the Soviet system, was already, in 1943, striving to depict the Roman Church as the friend of the Fascist aggressors and the foe of peace. It was a singular accusation; but in the excitement of war it gained some credence, and even official American opinion was concerned by the Pope's refusal to agree with Roosevelt that the Soviet tyranny was not so fundamentally inimical to religion as was Hitler's. It was also surprised by his dislike of the war aim of "unconditional surrender," agreed by the allies at the Casablanca Conference of 1943, an aim which seemed to Pius to be not only un-Christian but calculated to prolong the war by causing the beleaguered European central powers to fight to the last. . . .

PART TWO

The Papacy and the Jewish Question

Guenter Lewy
The Role of the Papacy in The
Jewish·Question

Born in Germany in 1923, Guenter Lewy left his native land
at the age of 15, emigrating first to Palestine and then to the
United States. He has taught political science at Columbia University, Smith College, and the University of Massachusetts at
Amherst. Professor Lewy spent two years of research for this
book in Roman Catholic diocesan archives in Germany (Passau,
Regensburg, Eichstatt, Hildesheim, Paderborn, and Aachen) but
he did not have access to Vatican archives. It should be noted,
too, that German Protestant churches are not included in his survey; nor are the churches—Protestant and Catholic alike—in
Austria, Czechoslovakia, and the countries annexed or occupied
by Germany during World War II.
Is Professor Lewy hesitant to pronounce judgment regarding
Pius XII's "silence" in 1943? To what extent does he concur
with Rolf Hochhuth's portrayal of Pius?

<hr>

SOURCE. Guenter Lewy, The Catholic Church and Nazi Germany (New
York and Toronto: McGraw-Hill Book Company, © 1964; First McGraw-Hill
Paperback Edition, 1965) , pp. 295–308 and notes on pp. 399–401. Reprinted by
kind permission of McGraw-Hill Book Company, New York, and Weidenfeld
& Nicolson, London. Footnotes renumbered.

In April 1933 a communication reached Pope Pius XI from Germany expressing grave concern about the Nazis' anti-Semitic aims and requesting the Supreme Pontiff to issue an encyclical on the Jewish question. The letter was written by the philosopher, Dr. Edith Stein, a Jewish convert to Catholicism and later known as Sister Teresia Benedicta a Cruce of the Order of the Carmelites.[1] Edith Stein's request was not granted. Nine years later, in August 1942, the Gestapo removed her from a Dutch monastery, where she had sought refuge, and sent her to Auschwitz to be gassed. The debate whether or not the Papacy could have prevented or should at least have vigorously protested the massacre of the Jews of Europe, of which Edith Stein was one of the victims, has been going on ever since and has acquired new vigor as a result of Hochhuth's play Der Stellvertreter.

In 1928 Pius XI had accompanied the dissolution of the missionary society, "The Friends of Israel," with a condemnation of anti-Semitism.[2] But once the Nazis were established in power, the Pontiff, like the German episcopate, seems to have limited his concern to Catholic non-Aryans. At the request of Cardinal Bertram the Papal Secretary of State in September 1933 put in "a word on behalf of those German Catholics" who were of Jewish descent and for this reason suffering "social and economic difficulties."[3] In the following years the Holy See repeatedly took issue with the Nazis' glorification of race, but the Jewish question specifically was never discussed. In 1934 the influential Jesuit magazine Civiltà Cattolica, published in Rome and traditionally close to Vatican thinking, noted with regret that the anti-Semitism of the Nazis "did not stem from the religious convictions nor the Christian conscience . . . but from their desire to upset the order of religion and society." The Civiltà Cattolica added that "we could understand them, or even praise them, if their policy were restricted within acceptable bounds of defense

[1] Cf. Hilda Graef, Leben unter dem Kreuz: Eine Studie über Edith Stein (Frankfurt a.M., 1954) , p. 130.
[2] Acta Apostolica Sedis, XX (1928) , p. 104, quoted in Luigi Sturzo, Nationalism and Internationalism (New York, 1946) , p. 46. On the dissolution of the society "Amici Israel" see Franz Rödel, "Der Papst und das 'Erkorene Volk Gottes'," Abwehrblätter, XXXVIII (1928) , pp. 88–89.
[3] Note of the Papal Secretariat of State to the German government, September 9, 1933, Documents on German Foreign Policy, C, I, doc. 425, p. 794.

against the Jewish organizations and institutions. . . ."[4] In 1936 the same journal published another article on the subject, emphasizing that opposition to Nazi racialism should not be interpreted as a rejection of anti-Semitism, and arguing—as the magazine had done since 1890—that the Christian world (though without un-Christian hatred) must defend itself against the Jewish threat by suspending the civic rights of Jews and returning them to the ghettos.[5]

Pius XI's encyclical *Mit brennender Sorge* of March 1937 rejected the myths of race and blood as contrary to revealed Christian truth, but it neither mentioned nor criticized anti-Semitism *per se*. Nor was anti-Semitism mentioned in the statement of the Roman Congregation of Seminaries and Universities, issued on April 13, 1938, and attacking as erroneous eight theses taken from the arsenal of Nazi doctrine.[6] On September 7, 1938, during a reception for Catholic pilgrims from Belgium, Pius XI is said to have condemned the participation of Catholics in anti-Semitic movements and to have added that Christians, the spiritual descendants of the Patriarch Abraham, were "spiritually Semites." But this statement was omitted by all the Italian papers, including *L'Osservatore Romano*, from their account of the Pope's address.[7]

The Vatican's criticisms of the new Italian racial legislation introduced in 1938 centered upon those parts which conflicted with the canon law's provisions concerning marriage. When Italian theaters and other public facilities in December 1938 began to exclude Jews, *L'Osservatore Romano* complained that these measures no longer merely aimed at the segregation of the Jews, but smacked of un-Christian persecution.[8] The *Civiltà Cattolica*

---

[4] *Civiltà Cattolica*, no. 2024, quoted in Daniel Carpi, "The Catholic Church and Italian Jewry under the Fascists (to the Death of Pius XI)," *Yad Washem Studies*, IV (1960), p. 51.

[5] Ibid., pp. 51–52.

[6] Cf. Yves M.-J. Congar, O. P., *Die Katholische Kirche und die Rassenfrage*, trans. W. Armbruster (Recklinghausen, 1961) , p. 69.

[7] The statement was first reported by *La Croix*, no. 17060, September 17, 1938. It is accepted as accurate by Sturzo, *Nationalism and Internationalism* (New York, 1946) , p. 47.

[8] No. 288 of December 13, 1938, reported by Bergen, December 13, 1938, PA Bonn, Pol. III, 22.

similarly objected to being claimed as an ally by the Fascist press extolling racial anti-Semitism. "As always," writes a well-informed recent student of the period, "the views of *Civiltà Cattolica* were in accord with those of the Pontiff, though it was clear that the Jesuit fathers had nothing against a moderate anti-Jewish policy in Italy."[9]

The elevation of Cardinal Pacelli to the Papacy in the spring of 1939 brought to the chair of St. Peter a man noted for his pro-German sentiments and diplomatic skill. Hochhuth's Pope possessed of "aristocratic coldness" and eyes having an "icy glow" is perhaps a bit stylized, but all biographers agree that Pius XII, in contrast to his predecessor, was unemotional and dispassionate, as well as a master in the language of diplomatic ambiguity. "Pius XII," recalls Cardinal Tardini, "was by nature meek and almost timid. He was not born with the temperament of a fighter. In this he was different from his great predecessor."[10] Whether Pius XI would have reacted to the massacre of the Jews during World War II differently from Pacelli is a question on which it is tempting to speculate, but to which no definite answer is possible.

That the Holy See had no intrinsic objection to a policy of subjecting the Jews to discriminatory legislation became again clear when in June 1941 Marshal Pétain's Vichy government introduced a series of "Jewish statutes." The cardinals and archbishops of France made known their strong disapproval of these measures. But Léon Bérard, the Vichy Ambassador at the Holy See, was able to report to Pétain, after lengthy consultations with high Church officials, that the Vatican did not consider such laws in conflict with Catholic teaching. The Holy See merely counseled that no provisions on marriage be added to the statutes and "that the precepts of justice and charity be considered in the application of the law."[11] In August 1941 the consequences of this discriminatory policy could not yet be clearly seen, but the episode illustrates anew the Vatican's willingness to go along with anti-Semitic measures, administered with "justice and charity."

[9] Richard A. Webster, *The Cross and the Fasces: Christian Democracy and Fascism in Italy* (Stanford, Cal., 1960) , p. 126.

[10] Tardini, *op. cit.*, p. 59.

[11] Quoted in L. Poliakov, *Harvest of Hate* (London, 1956) , p. 300.

When mass deportations from France got under way in 1942 the Papal Nuncio, without invoking the authority of the Holy See, requested Laval to mitigate the severity of the measures taken against the Jews of Vichy France,[12] but such pleas by that time could no longer halt the machinery of destruction.

Meanwhile, there was growing criticism of the Pope's failure to protest publicly against Nazi atrocities and especially against the murder of the Jews in the Polish death factories. Harold H. Tittman, the assistant to Roosevelt's personal representative at the Holy See, Myron C. Taylor, in July 1942 pointed out to the Vatican that its silence was "endangering its moral prestige and its undermining faith both in the Church and in the Holy Father himself."[13] After authorization by Secretary of State Hull, Tittman and several other diplomatic representatives at the Vatican in September 1942 formally requested that the Pope condemn the "incredible horrors" perpetrated by the Nazis. A few days later Taylor forwarded to the Papal Secretary of State, Luigi Maglione, a memorandum of the Jewish Agency for Palestine that reported mass executions of Jews in Poland and occupied Russia, and told of deportations to death camps from Germany, Belgium, Holland, France, Slovakia, etc. Taylor inquired whether the Vatican could confirm these reports, and, if so, "whether the Holy Father has any suggestions as to any practical manner in which the forces of civilized public opinion could be utilized in order to prevent a continuation of these barbarities."[14]

On October 10 the Holy See replied to Taylor's note that up to the present time it had not been possible to verify the accuracy of the severe measures reportedly taken against the Jews. The statement added, "It is well known that the Holy See is taking advantage of every opportunity offered in order to mitigate the suffering of non-Aryans."[15] In conversation with high-placed officials of the Curia, Tittman was told that the Pope's silence

---

[12] Abetz to the Foreign Ministry, August 28, 1942, PA Bonn, Staatssekretär, Vatikan, Bd. 4.

[13] Tittman to the Secretary of State, July 30, 1942, *U. S. Diplomatic Papers 1942*, III, 772.

[14] Taylor to Maglione, September 26, 1942, *ibid.*, p. 776.

[15] Tittman's summary of Holy See statement of October 10, 1942, ibid., p. 777.

was due to the following reasons: the desire of the Holy See to
maintain its absolute neutrality in the world-wide conflict, the
importance of Papal pronouncements standing the test of time
(which quality was difficult to achieve in the heat of the passions
of war and the errors resulting therefrom) and the fear that any
clearly pointed protest would worsen the situation of Catholics in
the Nazi-occupied countries. The Pope hesitated to condemn
German atrocities, Tittman also learned, because he did not
want to incur later the reproach of the German people that the
Catholic Church had contributed to their defeat.[16] After the
Western Allies in December 1942 had vigorously denounced the
cold-blooded extermination of the Jews, Tittman again inquired
from the Papal Secretary of State whether the Holy See could
not issue a similar pronouncement. Maglione answered that the
Holy See, in line with its policy of neutrality, could not protest
particular atrocities and had to limit itself to condemning immoral actions in general. He assured Tittman that everything possible was being done behind the scenes to help the Jews.[17]

Two days later, in the course of a lengthy Christmas message
broadcast over the Vatican radio, Pope Pius made another of his
many calls for a more humane conduct of hostilities. All men of
good will, the Pope demanded, should bring the life of the nations again into conformity with the divine law. Humanity owed
the resolution to build a better world to "the hundreds of thousands who, without personal guilt, sometimes for no other reason
but on account of their nationality or descent, were doomed to
death or exposed to a progressive deterioration of their
condition."[18] Addressing the Sacred College of Cardinals in
June 1943 the Pontiff spoke of his twofold duty to be impartial
and to point up moral errors. He had given special attention, he
recalled, to the plight of those who were still being harassed be-

[16] Tittman to the Department of State, October 6, 1942, ibid.; Tittman
dispatch of September 8, 1942, Department of State Papers, 740.00116 European War 1939/573, 1/2.

[17] Tittman to the Department of State, December 22, 1942, Department of
State Papers, 740.0016 European War 1939/689.

[18] Corsten, *Kölner Aktenstücke*, doc. 220, p. 280. The message was mimeographed and distributed in Germany by the diocesan chanceries. I have seen a
copy in DA Eichstätt.

cause of their nationality or descent, and who, without personal guilt, were subjected to measures that spelled destruction. Much had been done for the unfortunates that could not be described yet. Every public statement had had to be carefully weighed "in the interest of those suffering so that their situation would not inadvertently be made still more difficult and unbearable." Unfortunately, Pius XII added, the Church's pleas for compassion and the observance of the elementary norms of humanity had encountered doors "which no key was able to open."[19]

The precise nature of these interventions prior to June 1943 has not been revealed to this day. We do know that Nuncio Orsenigo in Berlin made inquiries several times about mass shootings and the fate of deported Jews. Ernst Woermann, the director of the political department of the German Foreign Ministry, on October 15, 1942, recorded that the Nuncio had made his representation with "some embarrassment and without emphasis."[20] State Secretary Weizsäcker told Monsignor Orsenigo on another such occasion that the Vatican had so far conducted itself "very cleverly" in these matters and that he would hope for a continuation of this policy. The Nuncio took the hint and "pointed out that he had not really touched this topic and that he had no desire to touch it."[21] Himmler, when received by Count Ciano on his visit to Rome in October 1942, praised the "discretion" of the Vatican.[22]

There were other diplomatic representations. That of the Nuncio in Vichy France has already been mentioned. In Slovakia, where 52,000 Jews had been deported in the spring of 1942, the Vatican in the summer of that year pointed out to the Quisling government, at whose head stood a Catholic priest, Dr. Josef Tiso, that the deported Jews had been sent away not for labor service, but for annihilation. The deportations ground to a halt, for Eichmann's emissary had instructions to avoid "political

[19] Pius XII to the Cardinals, June 2, 1943, excerpts in *AB Munich,* August 12, 1943.
[20] Memo of Woermann, PA Bonn, Staatssekretär, Vatikan, Bd. 4.
[21] Weizäcker to Woermann etc., December 5, 1941, quoted in Hilberg, *op. cit.,* p. 441.
[22] *The Ciano Diaries: 1939–1943,* ed. by Hugh Gibson (New York, 1946), p. 530.

complications." Thereafter, the Slovakian Jews lived in relative security until September 1944.[23] However, the case of Catholic Slovakia was a special one, and in the over-all balance one has to agree with the Pope's own finding that the Holy See was unsuccessful in opening the doors that barred relief for the hapless victims. But did the Holy See try all the keys in its possession?

The Pope's policy of neutrality encountered its most crucial test when the Nazis began rounding up the 8,000 Jews of Rome in the fall of 1943. Prior to the start of the arrests, the Jewish community was told by the Nazis that unless it raised 50 kilograms of gold (the equivalent of $56,000) within thirty-six hours, 300 hostages would be taken. When it seemed that the Jews themselves could only raise part of this ransom, a representative of the community asked for and received an offer of a loan from the Vatican treasury. The Pope approved of this offer of help, which, as it later turned out, did not have to be invoked.[24] But the big question in everyone's mind was how the Supreme Pontiff would react when the deportation of the Jews from the Eternal City began.

The test came on the night of October 15–16. While the roundup was still going on a letter was delivered to General Stahel, the German military commander of Rome. Bearing the signature of Bishop Hudal, the head of the German Church in Rome, it said:

"I have just been informed by a high Vatican office in the immediate circle of the Holy Father that the arrests of Jews of Italian nationality have begun this morning. In the interest of the good relations which have existed until now between the Vatican and the high German military command . . . I would be very grateful if you would give an order to stop these arrests in Rome and its vicinity right away; I fear that otherwise the Pope will have to make an open stand which will serve the anti-German propaganda as a weapon against us."[25]

A day later, Ernst von Weizsäcker, the new German Ambas-

[23] Poliakov, *op. cit.*, pp. 159–160; Raul Hilberg, *The Destruction of the European Jews* (Chicago, 1961) , pp. 469–470.

[24] Hilberg, *op. cit.*, p. 427; Renzo de Felice, *Storia degli ebrei italiani sotto il fascismo* (Torino, 1961), p. 527.

[25] Gumbert (of the German Embassy at the Quirinal) to the Foreign

sador at the Holy See, reported to Berlin that the Vatican was upset, especially since the deportations had taken place, as it were, right under the Pope's window:

"The people hostile to us in Rome are taking advantage of this affair to force the Vatican from its reserve. People say that the bishops of French cities, where similar incidents occurred, have taken a firm stand. The Pope, as supreme head of the Church and Bishop of Rome, cannot be more reticent than they. They are also drawing a parallel between the stronger character of Pius XI and that of the present Pope."[26]

Contrary to Hudal's and Weizsäcker's apprehensions, however, the man in the Vatican palace remained silent. On October 18, over 1,000 Roman Jews—more than two-thirds of them women and children—were shipped off to the killing center of Auschwitz. Fourteen men and one woman returned alive. About 7,000 Roman Jews—that is, seven out of eight—were able to elude their hunters by going into hiding. More than 4,000, with the knowledge and approval of the Pope, found refuge in the numerous monasteries and houses of religious orders in Rome,[27] and a few dozen were sheltered in the Vatican itself. The rest were hidden by their Italian neighbors, among whom the anti-Jewish policy of the Fascists had never been popular. But for the Germans, overwhelmingly relieved at having averted a public protest by the Pope, the fact that a few thousand Jews had escaped the net was of minor significance. On October 28 Ambassador Weizsäcker was able to report:

"Although under pressure from all sides, the Pope has not let himself be drawn into any demonstrative censure of the deportation of Jews from Rome. Although he must expect that his attitude will be criticized by our enemies and exploited by the Prot-

---

Ministry, October 16, 1943, PA Bonn, Inland IIg, 192. Bishop Hudal had signed this letter at the urging of several anti-Nazi officials in the German legations at the Quirinal and Holy See who had composed it. I have used the English translation of Hilberg, *op. cit.*, p. 429.

[26] Weizsäcker to the Foreign Ministry, October 17, 1943, PA Bonn, Inland IIg, 192. The translation is that of Poliakov, *op. cit.*, p. 297, n. 16.

[27] Cf. Robert Leiber, S.J., "Pius XII und die Juden in Rom 1943–1944," *Stimmen der Zeit*, CLXVII (1960–61), 429–430.

estant and Anglo-Saxon countries in their propaganda against
Catholicism, he has done everything he could in this delicate
matter not to strain relations with the German government and
German circles in Rome. As there is probably no reason to expect other German actions against the Jews of Rome, we can
consider that a question so disturbing to German–Vatican relations has been liquidated.

"In any case, an indication for this state of affairs can be seen
in the Vatican's attitude. *L'Osservatore Romano* has in fact
prominently published in its issue of October 25–26 an official
communiqué on the Pope's charitable activities. The
communiqué, in the Vatican's distinctive style, that is, very
vague and complicated, declares that all men, without distinction
of nationality, race or religion, benefit from the Pope's paternal
solicitude. The continual and varied activities of Pius XII have
probably increased lately because of the greater sufferings of so
many unfortunates.

"There is less reason to object to the terms of this message
. . . as only a very small number of people will recognize in it a
special allusion to the Jewish question."[28]

When an Italian law of December 1, 1943, provided for the
internment of all Jews in concentration camps and for the confiscation of their property, *L'Osservatore Romano* criticized these
measures as too harsh. But Weizsäcker reassured Berlin that
these "commentaries are not official. They have not been broadcast by the Vatican radio."[29] During the following months
searches for Jews took place periodically. The Pope, continuing
acts of charity, maintained his silence.

The criticism levelled against Pius XII for his failure to protest the massacre of the Jews of Europe, including those in his
own diocese of Rome, is composed of two main parts. It has
been argued first, most recently by Hochhuth, that the Pope
could have saved numerous lives, if not halted the machinery of

[28] Weizsäcker to the Foreign Ministry, October 28, 1943, PA Bonn, Inland
IIg, 192. The English translation is that of Poliakov, *op. cit.*, pp. 297–298, n.
16.

[29] Weizsäcker to the Foreign Ministry, December 3, 1943, PA Bonn, Pol. III,
22.

destruction, had he chosen to take a public stand and had he confronted the Germans with the threats of an interdict or the excommunication of Hitler, Goebbels and other leading Nazis belonging to the Catholic faith. As examples of the effectiveness of public protests it is possible to cite the resolute reaction of the German episcopate to the euthanasia program. In a number of other instances, notably in Slovakia, Hungary and Rumania, the forceful intervention of the Papal Nuncios, who threatened the Quisling governments with a public condemnation by the Pope, was able, albeit temporarily, to stop the deportations.[30] At the very least, it has been suggested, a public denunciation of the mass murders by Pius XII, broadcast widely over the Vatican radio and read from the pulpits by his bishops, would have revealed to Jews and Christians alike what deportation to the east entailed. The Pope would have been believed, whereas the broadcasts of the Allies were often shrugged off as war propaganda. Many of the deportees, who accepted the assurances of the Germans that they were merely being resettled, might thus have been warned and given an impetus to escape. Many more Christians might have helped and sheltered Jews, and many more lives might have been saved.

There exists, of course, no way of definitively proving or disproving these arguments. Whether a Papal decree of excommunication against Hitler would have dissuaded the Führer from carrying out his plan to destroy the Jews is very doubtful. A revocation of the Concordat by the Holy See would have bothered Hitler still less. However, a flaming protest against the massacre of the Jews, coupled with the imposition of the interdict upon all of Germany or the excommunication of all Catholics in any way involved with the apparatus of the Final Solution, would have been a far more formidable and effective weapon. It certainly would have warned many who were deceived by the Germans' promises of good treatment. Yet this was precisely the kind of action which the Pope could not take without risking the allegiance of the German Catholics. Given the indifference of the

---

[30] Cf. Hilberg, *op. cit.*, p. 539; Gerald Reitlinger, *The Final Solution* (New York, 1953), pp. 431–432. The successful intervention of the Papal Nuncio in Rumania was attested to by the former Chief Rabbi of Rumania at the Eichmann trial (cf. *New York Times*, May 24, 1961, p. 12).

German population toward the fate of the Jews, and the highly ambivalent attitude of the German hierarchy toward Nazi anti-Semitism, a forceful stand by the Supreme Pontiff on the Jewish question might well have led to a large-scale desertion from the Church. When Dr. Edoardo Senatro, the correspondent of *L'Osservatore Romano* in Berlin, asked Pius XII whether he would not protest the extermination of the Jews, the Pope is reported to have answered, "Dear friend, do not forget that millions of Catholics serve in the German armies. Shall I bring them into conflicts of conscience?"[31] The Pope knew that the German Catholics were not prepared to suffer martyrdom for their Church; still less were they willing to incur the wrath of their Nazi rulers for the sake of the Jews whom their own bishops for years had castigated as a harmful influence in German life. In the final analysis, then, as Poliakov has also concluded, "the Vatican's silence only reflected the deep feeling of the Catholic masses of Europe"[32]—those of Germany and eastern Europe in particular. The failure of the Pope was a measure of the Church's failure to convert her gospel of brotherly love and human dignity into living reality.

Some writers have suggested that a public protest by the Pope would not only have been unsuccessful in helping the Jews, but might have caused additional damage—to the Jews, to the *Mischlinge,* the Church, the territorial integrity of the Vatican and the Catholics in all of Nazi-occupied Europe. It is tempting to dismiss this argument by asking what worse fate could have befallen European Jewry than the disaster that did overtake it. Since the condition of the Jews could hardly have become worse, and might have changed for the better, as a result of a Papal denunciation, one could ask why the Church did not risk the well-being and safety of the Catholics and of the Vatican. Why did she not at least attempt to help the Jews?

The Catholic bishops of Holland tried this gamble. In July 1942, together with the Protestant Church, they sent a telegram of protest against the deportation of the Dutch Jews to the Ger-

[31] Statement of Dr. Senatro on March 11, 1963, at a public discussion in Berlin. Fritz J. Raddatz, ed., *Summa inuria oder Durfte der Papst schweigen?* (Reinbek bei Hamburg, 1963) , p. 223.
[32] Poliakov, *op. cit.,* p. 302.

man *Reichskommissar* and threatened to make their protest public unless the deportations were halted. The Germans responded by offering to exempt from deportation non-Aryans converted to Christianity before 1941 if the churches would remain silent. The Dutch Reformed Church agreed to the bargain, but the Catholic Archbishop of Utrecht refused, and issued a pastoral letter in which he denounced the wrong done to the Jews. The Germans retaliated by seizing and deporting all the Catholic non-Aryans they could find, among them the noted philosopher Edith Stein.[33] Once the inability of the Pope to move the masses of the faithful into a decisive struggle against the Nazis is accepted as a fact, there is thus some basis for the contention that a public protest, along with any good that would have come of it, might have made some things worse, if not for the Jews, at least for the *Mischlinge* and the Catholics themselves.

The silence of the Pope had other, perhaps still weightier, reasons. As Mr. Tittman was told by highly placed officials of the Curia, the Holy See did not want to jeopardize its neutrality by condemning German atrocities. The Vatican wanted to preserve its good name with the Germans, as well as with the Western Allies, and the Pope was unwilling to risk later charges that he had been partial and had contributed to a German defeat. Moreover, as already discussed in an earlier context, the Vatican did not wish to undermine and weaken Germany's struggle against Russia. In the late summer of 1943 the Papal Secretary of State, Luigi Maglione, termed the fate of Europe dependent upon a victorious resistance of Germany at the Eastern Front,[34] and Father Leiber, one of the secretaries of Pius XII, recalls that the late Pope always looked upon Russian Bolshevism as more dangerous than German National Socialism.[35] Hitler, therefore, had to be treated with some forebearance.

Finally, one is inclined to conclude that the Pope and his advisors—influenced by the long tradition of moderate anti-Semi-

[33] Louis de Jong, "Jews and non-Jews in Nazi-Occupied Holland," Max Beloff, ed., *On the Track of Tyranny* (London, 1960) , pp. 148–149.

[34] Reported by Weizsäcker, September 23, 1943, PA Bonn, Staatssekretär, Vatikan, Bd. 4.

[35] Robert Leiber, S.J., "Der Papst und die Verfolgung der Juden," Raddatz, *op. cit.*, p. 104.

tism so widely accepted in Vatican circles—did not view the plight of the Jews with a real sense of urgency and moral outrage. For this assertion no documentation is possible, but it is a conclusion difficult to avoid. Pius XII broke his policy of strict neutrality during World War II to express concern over the German violation of the neutrality of Holland, Belgium and Luxembourg in May 1940. When some German Catholics criticized him for this action, the Pope wrote the German bishops that neutrality was not synonymous "with indifference and apathy where moral and humane considerations demanded a candid word."[36] All things told, did not the murder of several million Jews demand a similarly "candid word"?

The discussion whether a Papal denunciation would have helped or harmed the Jews leaves untouched the one question that perhaps is the most compelling. It concerns the moral integrity of the Church, the performance of the Church as a guardian of the moral law. This second point at issue involves the Pope, the Bishop of Rome and Head of the Church, as much as all the other bishops called upon to provide moral leadership for their flock. In his first encyclical to the world, issued in October 1939, Pius XII described his duties as the Deputy of Christ in these words:

"As vicar of Him who in a decisive hour pronounced before the highest earthly authority of that day the great words: 'For this I was born, and for this I came into the world: that I should give testimony to the truth. Every one that is of the truth heareth my voice' (St. John xviii, 37), we feel we owe no greater debt to our office and to our time than to testify to the truth with Apostolic firmness: 'To give testimony to the truth.' This duty necessarily entails the exposition and confutation of errors and human faults; for these must be made known before it is possible to tend and to heal them. 'You shall know the truth and the truth shall make you free' (St. John viii, 32). In the fulfillment of this our duty we shall not let ourselves be influenced by earthly considerations nor be held back by mistrust or opposition, by rebuffs or

[36] Pius XII to the German bishops, August 6, 1940, copy in DA Regensburg.

lack of appreciation of our words, nor yet by fear of misconceptions and misinterpretations."[37]

Similarly the German bishops repeatedly affirmed their duty boldly to preach the word of God and fearlessly to condemn injustice. "The bishop," stressed Cardinal Faulhaber in 1936, "no longer would be the servant of God if he were to speak to please men or remain silent out of fear of men."[38] "I am aware," declared Bishop Galen in a sermon delivered in July 1941, "that as bishop, as harbinger and defender of the legal and moral order desired by God, which grants everyone basic rights and liberties not to be invaded by human demands, I am called upon . . . courageously to represent the authority of the law and to brand as an injustice crying to heaven the condemnation of defenseless innocents."[39] But these noble sentiments remained an empty formula in the face of the Jewish tragedy.

There were those within the Church cognizant of this failure. Writing under the impact of German atrocities in Poland and the defeat of France in June 1940, Cardinal Eugène Tisserant, a high official of the Vatican library, complained to Cardinal Suhard, Archbishop of Paris, that "our superiors do not want to understand the real nature of this conflict." He had pleaded with Pius XII, Tisserant said, to issue an encylical on the duty of the individual to follow the dictates of his conscience rather than blindly execute all orders, no matter how criminal.

"I fear that history will reproach the Holy See with having practiced a policy of selfish convenience and not much else. This is extremely sad, especially for those [of us] who have lived under Pius XI. Everyone [here] is confident that, after Rome has been declared an open city, members of the Curia will not have to suffer any harm; that is a disgrace."[40]

---

[37] Encyclical letter *Summi Pontificatus*, October 20, 1939, *International Conciliation*, no. 355 (December 1939), 556.

[38] Sermon on February 6, 1936, Faulhaber, *Münchener Kardinalspredigten*, 1st series, p. 17.

[39] Sermon on July 13, 1941, Heinrich Portmann, ed., *Bischof Galen spricht* (Freiburg, Br., 1946) , p. 49.

[40] Tisserant to Suhard, June 11, 1940, published from the files of the

Criticism of the Church's failure to offer unequivocal moral guidance could be heard also in Germany. The Jesuit Alfred Delp, a member of the German resistance, addressed a conference of priests at Fulda in 1943 and decried the fact that the Church had neglected to stand up for human dignity, the precondition of any Christian existence. "Has the Church," he asked, "forgotten to say 'Thou shalt not,' has the Church lost sight of the commandments, or is she silent because she is convinced of the hopelessness of her clear and firm preaching? Has the 'imprudence' of John the Baptist died out or has the Church forgotten man and his fundamental rights?"[41] The decisive question, Delp asserted on another occasion, is whether the Christians will be able and willing to stand up, not only for the Chruch and the Christian, but for man himself. The preoccupation with the question of the success or failure of bearing moral witness was in itself already a sign of moral corruption.[42] The silence of the Church on what was being done to the Poles and Jews and on the horrors committed in the concentration camps, Delp told a gathering of Bavarian churchmen in October 1943, threatened the acceptance of the Church by the new Germany that would arise after the downfall of the Nazi regime.[43] But Father Delp was an exceptional figure, whose vision transcended the institutional concerns of the Church. His counsel was not heeded.

Catholic theologians have long debated the dividing line between "Christian prudence" and "un-Christian cowardice." This line is often hard to locate, and no amount of casuistry about silence in the face of crime that is permissible in order to prevent worse will alleviate the arduous task of searching for it. Situations exist where moral guilt is incurred by omission. Silence has its limits, and that also holds true, as another German Jesuit had

German Reich Chancellery (BA Koblenz, R 43 II/1440a) by Eberhard Jäckel, "Zur Politik des Heiligen Stuhls im Zweiten Weltkrieg: Ein ergänzendes Dokument," *Geschichte in Wissenschaft und Unterricht*, XV (1964), 45. The letter was found and confiscated by the Germans during a search of the official residence of Cardinal Suhard in Paris.

[41] Alfred Delp, S.J., *Zwischen Welt und Gott* (Frankfurt a.M., 1957), p. 97.
[42] Ibid., pp. 293 and 233.
[43] Report on a talk by Delp at an "Informationskonferenz der bayerischen Ordinariate" in Munich on October 25, 1943, DA Passau.

reminded his Church as early as 1935, for the silence "to prevent worse." "For ultimately," wrote Father Pribilla, "the worst that could really happen is that truth and justice would no longer find spokesmen and martyrs on earth."[44] When Hitler set out on his murderous campaign against the Jews of Europe truth and justice found few defenders. The Deputy of Christ and the German episocopate were not among them. Their role gives a special relevance to the question the young girl in Max Frisch's *Andorra* asks her priest: "Where were you, Father Benedict, when they took away our brother like a beast to the slaughter, like a beast to the slaughter, where were you?"[45] This question still waits for an answer.

[44] Pribilla, *Stimmen der Zeit,* CXXVIII (1935) , 305.
[45] Max Frisch, *Andorra* in *Three Plays,* trans. Michael Bulloch (London, 1962) , p. 254.

John S. Conway
The Silence of Pope Pius XII

Born in London in 1929, John S. Conway is a Roman Catholic. He received his Ph.D. degree in history from Cambridge University in 1956 and is now professor of history at the University of British Columbia. His major publication is The Nazi Persecution of the Churches, 1933–45 *(London and New York, 1968), a book based primarily on documents in Hitler's Reich Chancellery, the various German government records, Nazi Party archives, and evidence produced for the Nuremberg trials. Professor Conway wrote the following article in rebuttal to some of the charges contained in Rolf Hochhuth's play,* The Deputy.

Does the author express an unqualified defense of Pius XII?

SOURCE. From John S. Conway, "The Silence of Pope Pius XII," *Review of Politics, XXVII,* No. 1 (January 1965) , pp. 105–131. By kind permission of the *Review of Politics* and the author.

It is hardly surprising that the play *Der Stellvertreter* (The
Deputy) by the young German author Rolf Hochhuth should
have aroused controversy ever since its first performance in February, 1963, in Berlin. For it aims to depict not merely historical
characters in a fictional drama, but historical characters in a historical setting of almost unprecedented significance and consequence. The use of the drama as a vehicle for political attack is
nothing new; but it is rare for the author to append, in the published version of his text, a historical essay of forty pages, seeking to give the evidence upon which his drama is based.[1] Nor is
it surprising that so pejorative is the portrayal in the play of the
late Pope Pius XII that many of those who served under him
during the nineteen years of his pontificate, as well as many others who came in touch with him through his literally thousands
of private or public audiences, have sought to come to his defense, in challenging the historical accuracy of Hochhuth's portrayal.

The most serious charge made by Hochhuth is that Pope Pius
XII remained silent throughout the whole process of the elimination of the European Jews by the Nazis, and thus could be
portrayed as a silent accomplice of the most dastardly crime of
the century. It is understandable that passions should be aroused
over such a tragic subject, and the implication that the whole
Church and not merely the Pope stood silent, has awakened
anew the mordant question of the relations between Jew and
Christian. Furthermore it has raised the more subtle but equally
significant issue of the role of the Church in the society of the
twentieth century, or, more particularly, the possibilities of its
political position in a continent beset by revolutionary forces and
totalitarian states.

The fact that Hochhuth is a German, that the play was first
produced in Germany, and that the crimes depicted were German crimes has also contributed to the controversy, since the
play is yet another attempt to force the Germans to face the facts

[1] The writer used the English edition of *The Deputy*. In London the
published play was entitled *The Representative* (1963). The writer would
like here to acknowledge indebtedness to the Alexander von Humboldt Foundation for a grant enabling him to visit Germany, to use German libraries,
and to pursue relevant sources.

of their immediate past, and has met with consequent resistance
from all those who are still unwilling to undertake this task. It
must be said at once that it is clearly not the author's intention to
make Pope Pius XII a scapegoat for German guilt, nor to seek
to detract from the enormities and atrocities committed in the
Nazi era. The length of the play made it necessary during its first
performance to cut out scenes which make clearer the author's
real intention of undertaking a thorough re-examination of the
past. Nevertheless the gravamen of Hochhuth's accusation
against the Pope needs to be examined for its historical rather
than its dramatic accuracy. And since the facts of the case are
more or less established, the concern of the historian is to study
the motives which lay behind the actions of the persons involved,
whether or not they can be used for popular drama or made the
object of a biting personal attack.

At the beginning, it should be pointed out that Hochhuth was
not the first to raise the question of the Pope's attitude towards
the Jewish persecutions under the Nazis or his personal relations
with the Nazi Government. In 1953 Gerald Reitlinger, in a book
now superseded, made the first attempt to document the persecution of the Jews, and wrote that the failure of Pope Pius XII to
protest against such crimes was to be ascribed not to subtle be-
nevolence nor to pro-German sympathies but to plain fear.[2] A
much more far-reaching attack was first produced in a book by a
Soviet Russian author, M. M. Scheinmann.[3] In three places he
specifically but rhetorically asked why no protest came from the
Vatican against the Nazi persecution of the Jews. Scheinmann's
book is notable for its assiduous culling of source material and
the utter perversity of its conclusions. According to Scheinmann,
Pope Pius XII was obsessed by one thought alone, the need to
organize a crusade against the Soviet Union, and he sought every
possible assistance for this purpose. In consequence the acts of
any anti-Soviet government, however criminal, were to be ignored or even approved. Various aspects of this "portrait" have
been taken over by Hochhuth, though he explicitly denies the

[2] Gerald Reitlinger, *The Final Solution* (London, 1953), pp. 353–357.
[3] The title in German translation is *Der Vatikan in Zweiten Weltkrieg* (E.
Berlin, 1954).

charge that the Vatican was seeking to organize a crusade against Bolshevism. Similar charges of "appeasement" towards Nazism appeared in other ephemeral pamphlets from the "democratic" left during the war years.[4]

It is a perhaps regrettable fact that Hochhuth has seriously weakened his historical case and, one might add, his dramatic achievement by overestimating the actual influence of the Papacy as an institution and by underestimating the actual character of the man, Pope Pius XII. Hochhuth turns the Pope into an ivory-towered and superficial opportunist, interested only in enlarging the finances of the Papacy and in spinning webs of diplomacy for his own satisfaction. His cold aristocratic laugh, the iron glow of his eyes, his disdainful mannerisms, and his all-too-carefully cultivated hands were supposed to contribute to the portrayal of a man who ignored the high calling of his office. Acquitting Pope Pius of the charge of being motivated solely by reasons of state, Hochhuth claims that he was no more than a "political neuter," an overzealous careerist, who later spent his time in useless games, while the tortured world waited in vain for a word of spiritual leadership.

This portrayal of cold inhuman skepticism provides Hochhuth with the chance of presenting the contrast with his hero, the Jesuit priest Riccardo, whose warm sympathy for the sufferings of his fellow men drove him to share the fate of the Jews in Auschwitz. It is consistent with Hochhuth's portrayal that he does not seek to depict Pius XII as being motivated by more positive reasons, whether political or religious. He is not shown as a violent political reactionary consumed with an anti-Communist hatred, as Scheinmann claimed, still less as a religious fanatic eagerly awaiting the destruction of the Jews as an opportunity to advance the Christian cause. Cold skepticism and inhumanity are supposedly reason enough for his silence.

The historical reality, however, was more complex. Quite apart from the extreme unlikelihood in the twentieth century that the head of the largest Christian Church in the world would be a man devoid of spiritual qualities, political intelligence, or the gift

[4] For example, Leo Lehmann, *Vatican Politics in the Second World War* (New York, 1945) .

of leadership, there exist many hundreds of witnesses to the contrary. Catholics and Protestants alike affirm that Pope Pius was a man of outstanding intelligence, devotion to the Church, and, as far as can be outwardly judged, spirituality.

It was hardly surprising that the Roman Catholic Church should have elected Eugenio Pacelli to be its Pontiff in the spring of 1939 when the storm clouds brooded so ominously over Europe, for there were aspects of his personal character which were particularly marked, and which indubitably contributed to his election. First, his chief qualification was his unrivalled diplomatic skill and his grasp of the political realites of the world scene. The British Ambassador, Lord D'Abernon, had described the Pacelli of the Berlin days as the most capable diplomat in the whole Berlin corps. He spoke seven languages fluently. For ten years he had been Cardinal Secretary of State and had devoted the closest attention to the darkening diplomatic scene.

At the time of his election to the Papacy in March, 1939, the ominous nature of the imminent political crisis was obvious to all. It was hardly an accident that the Church should seek as its leader for the troublous and difficult times ahead a man whose skill lay in the resolution of conflicts and the prevention of strife. The evidence would suggest that Pius XII also recognized this need. He shared the belief that the conflicts of the twentieth century were the outcome of violent nationalist policies which could only be overcome by the exercise of skillful and reconciling diplomacy. It was through the use of diplomacy rather than of prophetic utterance that the Pope hoped to achieve the aim of being able to seek peace and ensure it.

Second, as many witnesses agree, Pius XII had a clear concept of the vital need to promote peace. It was not merely a sentimental tribute, nor self-invented praise that, on his death, he was acclaimed as the Pope of Peace. Already in May, 1939, the German Ambassador to the Holy See, Bergen, noted that Pius XII had the desire to go down in history as a "Great Pope" and as a bringer of peace to the world.[5] After twenty-five years of

[5] *Documents of German Foreign Policy*, Series D, VI, no. 395. Later reference to these volumes will be given as *DGFP*. Even his name Pacelli symbol-

diplomatic experience, Pius XII was determined, wherever possible, to use the influence of the Papacy to achieve the peaceful settlement of outstanding disputes. On the other hand, his experience also taught him to evaluate carefully the difficulties of such a task. Throughout the first years of his pontificate, he was obliged to watch with increasing sorrow the lack of success of his efforts. Nevertheless, he was determined to explore what avenues were possible. Pope Pius deplored equally the devastations and disruptions which the conflicts of this century had brought with them. His aristocratic and cultivated background made him hostile to any attempt to overthrow the stability of church or state, and his whole cast of mind was opposed to egalitarian radicalism. It is not surprising that he was therefore totally opposed to the ideology of communism in which he saw only anarchism and barbarism. This impression was only strengthened by such experiences as that of 1919 in Munich when on the steps of the Nunciature a Communist put a pistol to Pacelli's head and threatened his life.

Finally, another personal characteristic of Pope Pius XII was the fact that he had lived for twelve years (1917–1929) in Germany, had close acquaintances among the German clergy, and was extremely well informed about all aspects of German life. It is undeniable that he was sympathetic to the German people, as his actions on their behalf after 1945 show. However, there is no evidence to believe that Pius XII was ever sympathetic to Nazism or still less to Hitler and his followers. Like most of the aristocratic German Catholics, he believed Hitler to be an upstart revolutionary from whom only the worst could be expected. Pope Pius was always reluctant to believe that the Germany he knew could be infected with the disease of Nazism, and unwilling to admit that the German people had so largely apostatized from their true beliefs. Throughout the Nazi era, Pope Pius suffered from this ambivalence of attitude towards Germany, though he

---

ized this desire, and his coat of arms contained a dove holding an olive branch. His first diplomatic assignment was to try and negotiate peace terms with the German Kaiser in 1917.

did not allow it to become a screen behind which to hide from the actual course of events in Germany, however distasteful, about which he was always extremely well informed.[6]

Before Hochhuth's interpretation of Pope Pius XII is accepted, or, alternatively, dismissed, it is necessary to examine in more detail and more thoroughly than Hochhuth has done, the actual historical circumstances of the time, and to see in their totality both the situation in which Pope Pius was called to act as a leader of the Church, and the decisions which he personally made in his dealings, as Cardinal Secretary of State and later as Pope, with the Nazi Government. Within three months of coming to power, in April, 1933, the Nazi leaders began negotiations with the Vatican for a concordat. Their object was to be able to suppress the last elements of "political Catholicism" as represented by the German Centre Party. They also wished to win international recognition from the Papacy and thereby to be acknowledged before the world as the rightful government of Germany and not just a revolutionary clique which had seized power. Papen, the Vice-Chancellor, and Göring, as Prime Minister of Prussia, were sent to Rome to take soundings with the Vatican's chief negotiator, Cardinal Pacelli.

These negotiations led to the signing of a concordat in July, 1933. Considerable doubts were raised on the Catholic side about the wisdom of this step. Following so hard on the virtual abandonment of democracy by the Reichstag's voluntary transfer of legislative power to Adolf Hitler in March, 1933, a move supported by the Catholic Centre Party, and on the German Catholic Bishops' removal of their prohibition of Nazi membership for Catholics, the Concordat appeared to many to be a further sign of the Catholic Church's adoption of expediency at the expense of principle. The accusation was later made, bitterly but perhaps not unexpectedly, by Brüning, the former leader of the Centre Party, that Pacelli in signing the Concordat betrayed the Catholic parliamentary group because of his desire for an authoritarian

---

[6] This did not of course prevent many ardent Nazis from denouncing him as lacking in sympathy for Germany, or other critics for being subservient to the political ideology of fascism.

Church controlled by the Vatican bureaucracy which could conclude an eternal alliance with an authoritarian state.[7]

The records of the German Foreign Ministry make it clear that Cardinal Pacelli was anxious to sign the Concordat for several clearly discernible reasons. In the first place, the Vatican had been seeking such an arrangement with the Weimar Republic for several years, and Pacelli himself had been responsible for the negotiations in Berlin. The Nazi Government was prepared to make concessions, on paper, far beyond those refused to the Church by the Republic. The Concordat would give the Church a new legal status, with corresponding advantages in the field of education, social welfare, and marriage laws. The position of the clergy would be substantially ameliorated.[8] In recognizing these advantages, Pacelli was under no illusion about the nature of the regime with which he was dealing. Already in August, 1933, the Cardinal had expressed himself very frankly in a conversation with a British diplomat, Ivone Kirkpatrick:

"His eminence was extremely frank and made no effort to conceal his disgust at the proceedings of Herr Hitler's Government. The Vatican usually professes to see both sides of any political question, but on this occasion there was no word of palliation or excuse. . . . Cardinal Pacelli equally deplored the actions of the German Government at home, their persecution of the Jews, their proceedings against political opponents, the reign of terror, to which the whole nation was subjected. I said to His Eminence that I had heard the opinion . . . that these events were but manifestations of the revolutionary spirit. With the passage of time, and the responsibilities of office Herr Hitler would settle down, temper the zeal of his supporters and revert to more normal methods of government. The Cardinal replied with emphasis that he saw no grounds for such easy optimism. It seemed

---

[7] Harry Graf Kessler, *Tagebücher 1918–37* (Frankfurt/Main, 1961), p. 742. Brüning himself voted for the Enabling Law on March 23, 1933. This issue has been raised again in the present controversy about the role of the Catholic Church in 1933, see H. Müller, *Katholische Kirche und Nationalsozialismus* (Munich, 1963), and C. Amery, *Die Kapitulation* (Hamburg, 1963).

[8] *DGFP*, Series C, Vol. I.

to him that there was no indication of any modification of the internal policy of the German Government."[9]

Asked why he had nevertheless signed a corcordat with such an iniquitous government, Pacelli replied that a pistol had been pointed at his head and he had no alternative. He had to choose between an agreement virtually on the lines desired by the German Government or the virtual elimination of the Catholic Church in the Reich. The Concordat provided a legal basis for Church life. "If the German Government violated the Concordat —and they were certain to do so—the Vatican would have a treaty on which to base a protest. In any case, the Cardinal added with a smile, the Germans would probably not violate all the articles of the Concordat at the same time."[10]

Pacelli's gloomy prognostications were all too soon fulfilled. The violent hostility of certain sections of the Nazi hierarchy was unrestrained, and despite the attempt of some German Catholics such as von Papen to serve both Hitler and God, such a compromise was impossible. By October, 1933, only three months after signing the Concordat, Pacelli complained to the German Foreign Ministry of "difficulties and persecutions, carried to a virtually intolerable degree, which the Catholic Church in Germany is now enduring in open violation of the Concordat."[11]

The Vatican was naturally kept well informed through both official and unofficial channels. Cardinal Pacelli was assisted in German affairs principally by three German priests, Prälat Ludwig Kaas, Father Robert Leiber, S.J., one of his closest advisors, and Father Walter Mariaux, S.J. It was they who carefully put together the ever-growing record of Nazi activities contrary to the Concordat and helped Pacelli to prepare the diplomatic notes to the German Government.[12] By 1937 the situation had grown

[9] *Documents of British Foreign Policy,* Second Series, V, no. 342.
[10] Idem.
[11] *DGFP,* Series C, II, no. 17.
[12] After the war some of these were published in Series C and D in whole or in part from the files of the German Foreign Ministry; others were printed for private circulation amongst the German Catholic hierarchy, *Dokumente betreffend die Verhandlungen zwischen der Hl. Stuhl and der Reichsregierung über die Ausführung des Reichskonkordat,* 3 Vols; also the Papal

so serious that the Vatican decided to make a public and most serious protest against the German Government's policies towards the Church, and to issue the famous Papal Encyclical *Mit Brennender Sorge,* read on Palm Sunday, 1937, throughout the Catholic Churches of Germany.[13]

Pacelli was naturally responsible for the contents of such protests even though he was obliged to recognize that satisfaction was far from obtained, that the Concordat continued to be widely and deliberately flouted, and that even the successful proclamation of the Encyclical did not deter Hitler from further actions against the Church. Nevertheless, he constantly strove to maintain the correct legal position against the radical illegality of the Nazi Party organs, and it is undoubtedly true that the Concordat did provide a basis for legality which gave to the Catholics a degree of protection which was, for example, notably lacking for Protestants.[14] There were always within the German governmental structure numerous bureaucrats who were also scandalized by the disregard for legality by Party officials. Further, the Roman Catholic Church was not embarrassed as were the Protestant Churches by the spectacle of overenthusiastic priests giving fervent support to the Nazi cause which was both unreciprocated and unwanted. Pacelli's efforts to protect the Catholic Church were not wholly successful. But it is certainly questionable whether a refusal to sign the Concordat in 1933 would have improved the situation. As it was, by 1939 the Vatican was obliged to acknowledge that the Nazi onslaught had succeeded in winning the loyalty of many Germans away from the Christian gospel. The fires of nationalism and the dream of world conquest lured many to follow the swastika in preference to the Cross.

The election of Cardinal Pacelli to the Pontificate in March, 1939, was not at all welcome to the Nazis, who had actively and openly campaigned for a candidate more sympathetic to their

---

notes of 1942–3, 3261–PS, 3263–PS, 3264–PS, *International Military Tribunal,* Vol. XXXII.

[13] For a partial English text, see A. S. Duncan Jones, *The Struggle for Religious Freedom in Germany* (London, 1938) , pp. 290–297.

[14] See the Allocution of Pope Pius XII to the Sacred College of Cardinals, June 2, 1945.

policies. Still less did they like the Pope's appointment of the pro-French Cardinal Maglione as his Secretary of State. But Hitler was not the man to allow such events to alter his plans. Only four days after Pius XII's coronation, the German aggression against Czechoslovakia was completed with the seizure of Bohemia and Moravia. According to the Italian Foreign Minister, Count Ciano, the new Pope was extremely concerned about this aggressive policy of the Germans. On the other hand he wanted to begin his reign with a conciliatory gesture and hoped that this would meet with an equally conciliatory reply. Otherwise what he could do would be reduced to a "vain soliloquy,"[15] for he was too newly installed in office to be able to take a firm line. As a result, a few days later the German Ambassador to the Vatican, Berger, reported that despite strong French pressure the Pope had refused to protest against "historic processes in which, from the political point of view, the Church is not interested."[16]

These events made the Pope realize the urgency of efforts to bring about some sort of settlement of outstanding differences. These efforts were necessary to secure the just and lasting peace, which was already his openly acknowledged goal. Mussolini's seizure of Albania on Good Friday, and the German take-over of Memel from Lithuania strengthened this consideration. In early May Pope Pius made soundings in London, Paris, Berlin, and Warsaw, as well as in Rome, for a possible five-power conference to take up those issues which seemed to the Pope most likely to be the causes of war, namely, the German-Polish quarrel and Franco-Italian relations.[17] Each government professed itself interested but unwilling to take the initiative, and two weeks later Hitler replied officially that, since there was no danger of war between Germany and Poland, he saw no real reason for an international conference. The reception of his initiative naturally disappointed the Pope.

He was forced to recognize that the chances for a successful intervention in the interests of peace could not be made by such a neutral power as the Papacy at a very early moment, since, as

[15] G. Ciano, *Diaries 1939–43* (New York, 1946), pp. 46–7.
[16] *DGFP*, Series D. VI, no. 65.
[17] *DBFP*, Series III, V, and *DGFP*, Series D, VI.

was the case in May, 1939, the urgency of the situation would not be recognized. Nevertheless, it would be equally inopportune to propose such an initiative at a late stage, after the powers had already so compromised themselves that they would feel unable to withdraw. Such indeed was to be the fate of Pope Pius' later efforts to induce the German and Polish governments to agree to a compromise solution at the end of August.[18] The Pope was obliged to stand on the sidelines after September 1, 1939, while Catholic marched against Catholic in the name of nationalism. And indeed his worst fears about the washing away of the stable landmarks of European civilization were to be all too fully realized, especially in the situation where the revolutionary forces of National Socialism and Soviet Communism had openly joined together in an alliance as unsavory as it was unwelcome.

The Pope's efforts for peace did not end with the outbreak of war. It was his continued desire to seek, if at all possible, to bring the hostilities to an end, or, at the very least, to limit them. Although he was deeply moved by the stories of the sufferings of the Polish people under the Nazi and Soviet onslaught, he could see no practical way to relieve them. The unwillingness of the Western Powers in 1939 to settle for a peace which would leave Poland in German hands was to be matched by the German certainty that during the next year Britain and France would come on their knees to beg for peace. Both sides refused to accept his suggestion for a truce at Christmas time, 1939. In an audience which the Pope gave to Ribbentrop in March, 1940, the arrogant certainty of the Nazi Foreign Minister crudely dismissed any talk of peace except on Germany's terms, or negotiations for that end through the Vatican. When the Pope turned the conversation to the condition of the Polish people, and expressed the desire to send an Apostolic Visitor there to organize relief work, Ribbentrop retorted that Poland was under military occupation and that diplomatic officials and consuls were not wanted there.[19]

Surprising as it may seem to those who accused the Pope of siding with Nazism, Pius XII refused to accept Ribbentrop's

---

[18] DBFP, Series III, VII, and DGFP, Series D, VII.

[19] DGFP, Series D, VIII, no. 668; A. Giovannetti, Der Vatikan und der Krieg (Cologne, 1961), pp. 178–90.

views on the certainty of a Nazi victory. At the very same time
the Vatican was also engaged in secret negotiations with representatives of the resistance groups within Germany, in particular
with the opposition group within the military leadership, with a
view to bringing about a negotiated settlement. During the winter
of 1939–1940, Dr. Joseph Müller, a Munich lawyer, travelled
several times to Rome to contact the Vatican and to put forward
the plans for a negotiated peace as formulated by this resistance
group. In particular, Dr. Müller was instructed to ask for the
Vatican's assistance in transmitting to the English and French
governments the opposition's request for a clear statement that
the Western Powers would be prepared to negotiate with a non-
Nazi government, if and when a plot to replace or displace Hitler
should succeed.[20] The fact that such negotiations were conducted in the Vatican could hardly have taken place without the
Pope's sanction, and is a clear indication that his sympathies
were so far antagonistic to the Nazi regime that he was willing to
lend his support to the efforts of the conspirators of the illegal
German opposition.[21]

The Pope's attitude towards Germany was openly different
from his public attitude towards the Soviet Union. When Germany attacked Poland, the *Osservatore Romano* commented:
"Two peoples are here crossing swords, spilling blood and starting a war over matters which ought to have rather been settled
peacefully," but three weeks later when the Soviet Union attacked Poland from the east, the Vatican protested loudly and
unequivocally against such a brutal aggression. Even more outspoken was the Papal condemnation of the Soviet aggression
against Finland in November, and December, 1939. The Pope
made special reference to Finland in his Christmas speech of
1939 and later condemned the Russian attack as the most cynical piece of aggression in modern times. The *Osservatore Romano* greeted with delight the exclusion of the Soviet Union

[20] For the details see *Vollmacht des Gewissens,* ed. by European Publications Society (Munich, 1960) and D. C. Watt, "Les Alliés et la Résistance
Allemande 1939–44" in *Revue de la deuxième Guerre Mondiale,* IX (1959),
65 ff.
[21] It is now apparent that these efforts failed because of the reluctance of
the highest military officers to engage themselves in the conspiracy.

from the League of Nations. In this case, there was no reluctance to take a firm stand, no talk of diplomatic neutrality or even of the need to protect those Catholics who were now under Russian control.

Such remarks stand in strong contrast to the comparative silence with which the Nazi invasion of Denmark and Norway was greeted. On the other hand, the Pope was moved to a most unusual and undiplomatic gesture on May 10, 1940, when he sent a telegram to each of the rulers of Belgium, Holland, and Luxemburg to assure them of his concern for their welfare, though here again there was no explicit condemnation of the German aggression.[22] After June 22, 1941, the Vatican's situation was only made more difficult in that any move or criticism which the Pope might make of Nazi crimes would only react in favor of the Communists of the Soviet Union, against whose ideology the Papal Encyclical *Divini Redemptoris* of Pope Pius XI had taken a very definite stand twenty years earlier. It was the impression of an American diplomat in the Vatican at the end of June, 1941, that the Papacy was keeping a "strict reserve" equidistant from Communist Russia or Nazi Germany. "The militant atheism of the former is still regarded as more obnoxious than the modern paganism of the latter."[23] Undoubtedly the Pope believed or, at any rate, hoped that the Germany he knew could be rescued from Nazism. Communism presented a much more fundamental ideological danger to the Church and to Christianity. It is hardly surprising that the German Ambassador to the Vatican could report on the very day of Germany's invasion of Russia that "in actual fact, his (the Pope's) warm sympathies for Germany and his desire not to complicate the already difficult situation impelled him to very far-reaching reserve."[24]

The outbreak of total war, the seeming impossibility of limiting its range, and the knowledge of the sufferings which such a war would entail, grieved the Pope immensely. In June, 1940, he was unable to prevent even his own beloved Italy from joining

[22] For the text, see C. M. Cianfarra, *The Vatican and the War* (New York, 1944), p. 225.

[23] W. Langer and R. Gleason, *The Undeclared War* (New York, 1953), p. 547.

[24] *DGFP*, Series D. XII, no. 674.

in.[25] The extra burdens which the war imposed on the Church, the moral and spiritual trials of clergy and laity alike, and the grievous attacks upon the Catholic position in almost every European country also were the cause of great concern. With feeling could the Pope write privately to the Bishop of Berlin in April, 1943:

"Seldom has the Holy See had to undergo such trials as at the present time. Our honest attempt has been to meet all the terrible conflicts which are engulfing the powers of the world with complete neutrality and yet at the same time to defend carefully the needs of the Church. And, as you rightly said, this trial is only made more difficult by the terrible atrocities and sins which the war has brought about. The seemingly limitless cruelty of the war machines makes the thought of a long drawn-out period of mutual slaughter unbearable. And what we have heard, day in and day out, of atrocities which are far beyond anything which could be ascribed to the necessities of war, is even more horrifying and shocking."[26]

There can be little doubt that the Pope was kept well informed of the extent of these atrocities both against Catholics and against Jews. Members of the clergy, the armed forces, and even some civilians who had been in Poland after the Nazi conquest, returned with countless stories of atrocities which were passed on to Rome.[27] Foreign governments sent similar information to the Vatican on a continuing basis.[28] And the Polish Government in exile kept the Vatican supplied with reports of happenings in Poland.

These dispiriting reports and the constant impression of tales of horror made the Pope eager to search for some part of the Church's life which could afford a ray of hope. Pope Pius' sup-

[25] See for his messages to Mussolini, *I Documenti Diplomatici Italiani,* Ninth Series (1939–43) , IV, nos. 189 and 232.
[26] *Petrus Blatt,* Organ of the Catholic Church in Berlin, March 3, 1963.
[27] In January, 1940, the Polish Cardinal Hlond published an extensive memorandum of the German crimes committed in Poland from September, 1939.
[28] See the letters from the U.S. Government, *Foreign Relations of the United States 1942,* III (Washington, 1961) , 772 ff.

porters argue that this statements of praise of Ireland and Spain for their staunch loyalty to the Catholic faith, which caused such dismay in democratic countries, are to be understood in this context. These countries were isolated examples of peace and stability, which had resisted the temptation to join the war despite the enormous pressure exerted upon them. Similarly, the restructuring of the government in France under Pétain, and the abrogation of the anticlerical laws of the Third Republic, could be greeted by the Vatican as evidence of a desire to seek stable government on Christian principles. These, however, were no more than scraps of silver linings on the very dark clouds which covered the rest of the world's horizons.

No one can judge how heavy was the burden of responsibility which the Pope had to carry. The awful consequences of his own position and actions were certainly only too clearly recognized. Pius XII was never given to easy optimism and his concentration on the conduct of affairs in his own hands compelled him to see the state of the world and the Church in all its horror and difficulty. He was naturally depressed that no one among the combatants paid any attention to his peace proposals, as contained in his Christmas messages during the first four years of the war. With sorrow he had to recognize that the influence of the Church, both as a source of moral and spiritual power for the individual, and as a supranational agency for peace, steadily declined.

The seeming ineffectiveness of the Christian faith in such a world was a heavy tribulation to have to bear. The attitude of the Papacy towards these events was therefore the result of long and difficult deliberation. In no sense could Pope Pius' abstention from outspoken protest be ascribed to ignorance of what was happening, to an opportunistic evaluation of possible gains for the Church, to deliberate complicity with Nazi ideals, or to the desire for financial gain. The ascription of such superficial motives to the Pope, as in the case of Hochhuth's play, stems from the playwright's failure to grasp the much deeper dilemma and crisis which the Pope had to face, or to examine the more positive reasons for the Pontiff's attitude throughout the war years.

The real crisis of conscience which the Pope had to face

throughout the whole wartime period was how to seek to redeem
the failure of the world to recognize the overriding necessity for
peace. War is sinful, and it was the prime responsibility of the
leader of the Roman Catholic Church to witness against sin, and
so to maintain, uphold, and encourage his followers that the
Church could play a full and effective role in overcoming this
sin. So too the Church must minister to the needs of those over-
whelmed by the catastrophes of war and uphold the ideals of
peace, righteousness, and freedom. Condemnation of the disas-
ters, crimes, and sinfulness of war had to be matched with a positive program for witnessing to the Christian faith, for strength-
ening the moral resources of the faithful, and for guarding and
upholding the barriers against immorality, which, as all knew
well, could fall away so easily in times of stress and trouble.

The Pope's problem was how to maintain the authority of the
Holy See, both as the spiritual guardian of faith and morals for
members of the Church, and as a significant diplomatic organization, whose voice and policy would be respected even by those
governments and peoples who acknowledged no allegiance to the
Church. How to make an effective contribution to the lessening
of the sufferings and sorrows of men and to the re-establishment
of peace was the constant question before the Pope. It is not yet
sufficiently realized how often the two ends were, or seemed to
be, mutually irreconcilable. The flow of evidence concerning the
outrages done in the name of Germany made this dilemma
worse. Would a forceful and undiplomatic Papal protest against
these atrocities serve to lessen, or only to increase, the crimes
committed by the Germans? Should the Pope openly proclaim
the rights of all men, of whatever race or religion, and denounce
in the sharpest possible way the manner in which such rights
were being ignored or trampled upon? Would not such a protest
have serious consequences, not merely for the Catholic Church
and its supporters, but for the victims themselves? On the other
hand, should he keep silent for fear of stirring up worse trouble?
Or would not such silence jeopardize the prestige of the Church
and raise doubts about the readiness of the Vatican to witness to
the moral values of which it was the acknowledged guardian?

All the Pope's speeches, his letters, and the reports of his interviews throughout the war make it clear that the weighing up

of such considerations, the careful balancing of one factor against another, the counteracting demands of his spiritual and of his temporal roles, the need to take some action and the impossibility of predicting what action would serve the cause of the Church best, were his daily preoccupations. Pope Pius was too clear-sighted not to recognize the all too likely eventualities of both action and lack of action. Yet it was not merely due to hesitation and doubt that in the end he decided to keep silent. Rather, this silence stemmed from thoughts and calculations, not reached lightly or frivolously, but only as the result of deep conviction and careful consideration.

Three main considerations would seem to have been uppermost in the mind of the Pope as he wrestled with this difficult and challenging responsibility. In the first place he was determined to seek every opportunity for reaching a peaceful settlement of the international conflicts. He recognized that the Vatican's diplomacy had suffered a striking setback with the unsuccessful attempt to prevent the outbreak of war. It was vitally necessary to seek to restore the probity of the Vatican's diplomacy in order to become once again a possible diplomatic vehicle for the negotiation of peace. In order to do this it was necessary to maintain the strictest neutrality between the warring countries. Accustomed as he was to the propaganda activities of governments, the Pope was well aware how readily any Papal pronouncement would be used as a weapon by one side or the other.[29] His experiences during the First World War also convinced him that only neutrality could maintain the basis of confidence that could be the basis for any Papal negotiation for reconciliation.

The desire of both sides to enlist the Papacy as an ally had to be strictly rejected;[30] yet not in such a way that recriminations could later be made or support given to either opponent.[31] In

[29] See Monsignor A. Giovannetti, Der Vatikan und der Krieg, p. 254.

[30] See the Pope's remarks on this subject to the College of Cardinals, Christmas, 1943.

[31] According to the American diplomat, H. H. Tittman, one of the motives, "possibly the most compelling," for the Pope's refusal to condemn the Nazi atrocities was his fear that "if he does so now, the German people, in the bitterness of their defeat, will reproach him later for having contributed, if only indirectly, to this defeat," as had happened to Benedict XV. "When it is

particular contrast to the behavior of the Churches in the First World War, Pope Pius XII was determined to prevent himself from being put in the position of an army chaplain, or to lend any religious support to the war effort. When in Italy men were eagerly debating the "religious nature of this war," Pope Pius refused to give the slightest blessing to Mussolini's ambitions. Similarly, despite strong pressure, even temptation, he refused to describe the war against Soviet Russia as a crusade. The Vatican refused to recognize the German conquests after 1939 as final. Even the religious polemic of the Vatican against Communism was curtailed almost to nothing after 1941.[32] The Pope was well enough aware of the tremendous damage done to the Church by its all-too-public activity in the First World War in blessing the guns of the opposing armies. It followed that silence was here a positive and deliberate policy in the interests of preserving neutrality and of preventing spiritual compromises of inestimable and catastrophic consequence.

The second reason for silence and the lack of protest was the conscious knowledge of the consequences which might follow both inside Germany and abroad. In the first place, the stronger the protest was, the more ammunition it would provide for the anti-Nazi cause. Even if it was hardly possible that the Nazi regime would desire to use the Papacy as a means of seeking peace, nevertheless there were strong reasons against a deliberate policy of abandoning the Vatican's neutral stand, of cutting off the Pope's last remaining hopes of influencing German policy, and of throwing his support to the anti-German side, particularly at a time when Italy and Germany were still allied.[33] Further-

---

borne in mind that Pius XII had many years of conditioning in Germany, it will not seem unnatural that he should be particularly sensitive to this particular argument." *Foreign Relations of the United States 1942*, III, 777.

[32] See also the difficulties posed for the Vatican by the Japanese desire to establish a diplomatic mission in early 1942 at the height of their military aggression, ibid., pp. 778–91.

[33] On the other hand, the reasons still have to be elucidated why Hitler in the summer of 1943 should have appointed as Ambassador to the Vatican, the most experienced diplomat in Germany, State Secretary Ernst von Weizsäcker. Since the explanation in Weizsäcker's memoirs is palpably inadequate, it can only be presumed that Hitler wanted to keep open this possible channel for negotiations for a future peace.

more, a strong anti-German protest might very well have had the result of inducing certain other countries to give in to the Allies' pressure to join in against Germany, and thus involve still more peoples in the catastrophes of war.

But these consequences were less serious than those which might and in all probability would follow in Germany itself. By 1940 Pope Pius entertained no illusions about the true nature of the Nazi regime. Temporary alleviations of the Church struggle within Germany, he rightly saw, were due not to Papal notes but only to tactical changes of emphasis in the Nazi plans, and preoccupation with their foreign conquests.

The Pope could not overlook the effects of the previous Papal protest, *Mit Brennender Sorge*. After this had been secretly smuggled into Germany in March, 1937, it had been distributed to every Catholic church without a single case of betrayal to the Gestapo. In the Nazi hierarchy, as recorded by the officials of the Foreign Ministry, the Encyclical was treated as a call to battle. Within two days of its proclamation, the Encyclical was banned, its printers arrested, and every available copy seized. At the end of the month, Hitler ordered that measures were to be initiated to dissolve the Catholic youth organizations and to amalgamate them into the Hitler Youth. On April 5 the Foreign Ministry noted that the police had taken severe (and illegal) action against individual priests and also against the Catholic press. On April 6, Hitler ordered a resumption of the trials of priests and monks on charges of immorality and of violations against the foreign currency laws. By the end of June, it was noted that Hitler was looking for still stronger action against the Church and the Concordat. Four or five of the more important articles of the Concordat were to be declared intolerable and no longer binding on Germany. It might be necessary to consider revoking the whole of the Concordat. On August 26, agreement was reached in the government Ministries that there should be the earliest possible dispatch and publication of a diplomatic note to the Vatican concerning the revocation of the Concordat, and that immediately thereafter a new Reich School Law should be promulgated with provisions for its execution which no longer took into account the safeguards of the Concordat.[34]

---

[34] *DGFP*, Series D, I, nos. 638, 640, 641, 642, 661, 677.

As another sign of the Nazis' increased hostility against the Churches, in July, 1937, the well-known Protestant Pastor Martin Niemöller was arrested and placed in protective custody. Pope Pius could draw little comfort from such a course of events. Nor had the German people, even the German Catholics, shown themselves, after the Nazi aggression was launched in total war, more willing to resist the Nazi appeal. On the contrary, they were only too willing, even the Catholic bishops, to praise Hitler for his successes in overthrowing the established order in Europe regardless of the cost in human lives that this entailed.

Nevertheless, it was still possible to hope that the legal status of the Church as outlined in the Concordat and the legal basis of German society could be used as weapons against the radical and anarchic illegality of the Nazi actions. This was seen in the case of the successful protests against the Nazi program of euthanasia, in particular the protests of the Bishop of Münster, Graf von Galen. In this issue the inmates of asylums had been put to death almost under the eyes of their relatives, who were thus at once informed both of the fact of their death and the probable manner. The protest which such action aroused was widespread enough to include even Nazis. Cardinal von Galen was thus the spokesman of a widely felt reaction against certain immediate and demonstrable crimes. The question which the Pope had to decide was whether a protest about other crimes, such as the much more secret atrocities against the Jews, would make the same appeal to legality, and receive sufficient response within Germany to make Hitler think again. Reluctantly the Pope had to admit that this was not the case.

His view that a protest might only cause worse misfortunes was strengthened by the violent course of events that swept over Holland in the summer of 1942. On July 26, the Dutch bishops issued a pastoral letter making clear their protest against the transportation of Dutch Jews out of Holland and in the direction of Poland. On August 2, as a direct reply, the Gestapo issued orders that all non-Aryan members of Dutch monasteries and nunneries were to be arrested. On the same afternoon the well-known German philosopher, Dr. Edith Stein, who had joined the Carmelite Order and had been placed for protection in a Dutch closed convent, was arrested. The Gauleiter, Schmidt, in a public broadcast stated that such actions were the result of the disloyalty of the bishops. On August 9 Edith Stein was murdered in Auschwitz.

The same conviction of the need to avoid making matters worse, sprang from consideration of events in Poland. The situation of the Church in Poland was a particular concern of the Pope's from the beginning of the war. How could the fate of the Polish people under German rule be remedied? Every attempt to persuade the Nazi authorities that the Concordat should also apply to Poland was rebuffed. Both the Papal Nuncio and the State Secretary in the Foreign Ministry, von Weizsäcker, were in agreement that open protests would only have made the situation worse. The position was notoriously bad in the Warthegau, that part of Poland which the Nazis decided to Germanify at all costs, and in which they carried on sharp persecution of all the Churches. Writing to the Bishop of Berlin in 1943, the Pope remarked:

"Hardest hit, as you know, is the Catholic Church in the Warthegau. We suffer much from the unending sorrows of the faithful there, all the more since every attempt to intervene for them with the government has been rejected brutally. The consequences of which we spoke earlier, in the special case of the Warthegau and above all the fear of endangering the rest of the pastoral care which is still allowed there, has held us back from speaking out about the present state of the Church in that area."[35]

Such considerations about the wisdom of an open protest and such fears of the consequences which might react on the heads of Hitler's victims led the Pope to give in the same letter more general advice along the same lines.

"We leave it to the bishops who are locally responsible to weigh up whether and how far there is a danger of reprisals or other pressures in case of episcopal protests. So too other considerations about the length and psychology of the war may make it

[35] *Petrus Blatt, loc. cit.* Two diplomatic notes from the Vatican protesting about the conditions in the Warthegau are reprinted as 3263–PS and 3264–PS, see note 12 above. They were politely but firmly refused by Weizsäcker on the grounds that since the Vatican did not recognize the German conquests in the East, the Nuncio could have no right of representation with regard to events in those areas.

more advisable, despite the many grounds to the contrary, to maintain a far-reaching reserve, *ad maiora mala vitanda* (in order to avoid worse consequences). Herein lies one of the reasons why we have ourselves been extremely limited in our pronouncements; and the experience we had in 1942 with such Papal publications as were given out to the faithful, as we see it, justifies our present attitude.''[36]

The third main reason why the Papacy kept silent was the uncertainty of the effects of such a protest inside Germany. Thought had to be given to the technical problem of how such a protest was to be made available to the German people in a situation where no public means of communication could be used, when the Church press was either suppressed or entirely controlled, and when even the movements of individual priests travelling to and from Rome were under constant surveillance. Few Germans were able to listen to the Vatican radio.[37] The private circulation of any document would have put every individual who handled it into grave danger; and the verbal broadcasting of such a protest would have reached only a tiny proportion of the population, even if those who heard it had been able to assure themselves of its reliability. In order to be effective, a protest about such a critical subject as the Nazi crimes against the Jews, would not only have to be widely received but widely believed.

Yet the very nature of the case prevented the possibility of the Vatican being able to obtain exact details of definite crimes, except from sources hostile to the Germans. Were such a protest to be based on such sources, it must be feared that few Germans would have accepted the facts as correct, so enthralled were they by Goebbels' rhetoric. Furthermore the question arose as to what would be achieved by such an unsubstantiated protest, however

[36] In August, 1942, the American Chargé noted the same far-reaching reserve among the Vatican officials. Although he pointed out that this might endanger the prestige of the Holy See, the answer was invariably that the Pope had already condemned offenses against morality in wartime, and that to be specific now would only make matters worse. Telegram of Tittman, July 30, 1942, in *Foreign Relations, 1942*, p. 772.

[37] On the other hand the Nazis threatened reprisals against the Catholics if the Vatican Radio "interfered" in political affairs to the extent of broadcasting the names of German prisoners-of-war in Russia.

sharply worded. It must be remembered that the majority of Germans, including Catholics, were convinced of the rightness of Hitler's campaign against Bolshevism. Even if they would admit that in the course of such a struggle, crimes had been committed, they were in no way ready to be convinced that these were the express desire of the highest organs of the Party, or that Hitler had personally ordered their execution. Since, despite Hitler's open statement of his intention to "deal with" the Jews, documentary details of his plans for their total extermination were never forthcoming, the awakening of the German public conscience, which would have been a necessary precondition for a successful protest, was simply out of the question.

On the other hand, the Pope was well enough aware that the destruction of the Jews, which added nothing to the successful propagation of the German war effort, was an issue of crucial importance to Hitler and his immediate followers. A defense of the Jews would indeed have been a direct attack on the whole ideology of Nazism and the attempt to found "the thousand-year Reich." There was no likelihood of being able to persuade Hitler to abandon such a program for tactical reasons. It would be necessary to weigh up therefore whether Hitler could be persuaded or obligated to discontinue this persecution because of the likely political reaction from within Germany itself. But for the Papacy to challenge the Nazi power directly on a matter of such crucial significance would have raised in an inescapable form for each German Catholic the question of loyalty to one or other set of values. It is quite untrue to suggest that the majority of German Catholics were only waiting for such a sign from the Papacy to throw off their allegiance to the Nazi creed. Certainly, the German bishops, priests, and laity could have tried to raise the same storm of protest as they had already done about the euthanasia operations.

It is significant that no such widespread protest against the anti-Semitic persecutions came from within Germany itself. Indeed, it was all too true, that anti-Semitism had infected large numbers of the German Catholics to the point where they would have refused to understand, let alone to respond, to any leadership from the Pope. All too many Catholics hailed with delight the public actions of the Nazis against the Jews, and accepted as true the Nazi propaganda which directly contradicted the teaching of the Church.[38] Such phenomena reveal only too clearly the corruption of the German mind, the refusal to think rationally, only emotionally, about the Nazi theories of race and blood and the almost universal trend in Germany to excuse anti-Semitism as a minor example of overenthusiasm not to be compared in importance with the victories won for Germany by the Nazi leaders.

The evidence suggests that the Vatican knew well enough that without systematic preparation of the Church's case, it would be impossible to convince millions of Germans by a single protest, or a series of protests, of the iniquity of the actions of their rulers, actions of which the vast bulk of the population was up to that time to a greater or lesser extent deliberately ignorant. Without such advance preparation and information, a protest would only have led to confusion and schizophrenia among the faithful. Yet at this distance of time, there remain the inescapable questions: Why the Vatican never began to undertake this task of preparation and information and why it should have believed that the consciences of the faithful were of such importance that they should not be faced with the requirements of the Christian Gospel? Yet, even if the Vatican had attempted such a task, there is little evidence that the German Catholics would have responded. While it is difficult to try and assess such an incalculable factor in the minds of the Germans in the midst of the wartime situation, the observer cannot help raising the critical question of how many of those who today believe, like Hochhuth, that the Pope should have denounced the Nazi persecution of the Jews, would have actively followed his lead, if he had spoken out.

Furthermore, a protest would have to have been more than a mere dissemination of information. It had to be a call to action. In that case, any German Catholic who responded to the Pope's appeal and who refused any longer to serve the Nazis would have been in the eyes of the Nazis, and in the eyes of the majority

---

[38] The same was true of course for Polish Catholics. The contrast with the situation in Denmark, where anti-Semitism was almost nonexistent, and where the population did all it could to protect the Jews, is illuminating.

of the population, guilty of high treason. The grim thoroughness with which such "traitors" were dealt after July 20, 1944, is proof enough that such a revolt, even if the German Catholics had been ready and willing to carry it out, would have hardly deterred Hitler from executing his plans against the Jews.

If the Pope had limited himself to informing his faithful followers of the events and crimes which lay so much upon his conscience, he would thereby have laid upon each individual member the guilt of association and weighed down the consciences of priest and people alike. Not only would such an action have been quite untraditional in the Catholic Church, but it could hardly have led to better results. For the experience of the Nazi era, even before the outbreak of war, proved conclusively that the individual was completely powerless to protest against the massive organized power of the State. It was only possible to oppose the Nazi regime through some form of organization, and by 1939 the only undirected organizations left in Germany were the Christian Churches. But after the years of the Church struggle, and in the midst of a war, which everyone accepted as being fought for national survival, the Catholic Church was not in a position to undertake the task of forcing its members to choose between Church and State. The authority of the Papacy was never, indeed never could be, dogmatically or politically of such strength.

It is therefore quite untrue to suggest that the Pope was in a position to force the thirty-five million German Catholics to rise up and oppose Hitler's persecution of the Jews. To say this is completely to misunderstand the situation. For although some Catholics undoubtedly knew of the existence of concentration camps and rumors were current of the illegal actions which took place there, the actual extermination camps were not in Germany proper, the majority of the victims were not Germans, and few Germans knew them personally. Even the German Jews had for years before been the victims of a process of isolation by which their contacts with other Germans were cut off. If they were deported, few knew where they had gone, still less what had happened to them. No one had, or wanted to have, any certain information that a systematic extermination was actually being carried out on the orders of Hitler himself. Even if the

German population had been eager and willing to protest, and they were not, it must be questioned how such a protest could have been organized against crimes about which no certain details, figures, names, or dates were known.

It is small wonder, therefore, that the Pope should have declared to the College of Cardinals on June 2, 1943: "Every word which we have sent to the respective authorities about such matters, and each of Our public pronouncements must be the object of long and thoughtful deliberation in the interests of the suffering peoples themselves, lest involuntarily their position should be made even worse, more difficult and unbearable."[39] The only possible avenue of positive aid which the Pope could see was to try and extend assistance on the local level, and in isolated instances this could be all the more effective for not seeming to call in question the whole authoritarian power of the Nazi state. And yet, on the same day, October 16, 1943, that the Gestapo ordered the first deportation of Jews from Rome, the Pope did not intervene. The protests presented by the Rector of the German Catholic College to the German military commander, General Stahel, came from the outraged members of the German community. On the other hand, thousands of Jews remained hidden and safe in one hundred and fifty-five Catholic houses, monasteries, and institutions throughout the city.[40] Similarly the protests of the Papal Nuncios in Hungary and Slovakia, which contributed to the prevention of deportations of Jews, were only effective for being taken on the local level, and with non-German governments—though it should not be forgotten that it was a Catholic priest, Monsignor Tiso, who, as Premier of Slovakia, made it his boast that his country would be the first to be completely purged of the evil taint of Jewry. The postwar tributes paid to the Pope by Jews and Gentiles alike for his efforts on their behalf can hardly be dismissed as meaningless.

If these were the positive reasons that led Pope Pius XII to keep silent in the face of crimes unprecedented in their

---

[39] Quoted in W. Bussmann, "Der Papst und die Diktatur," in *Monat*, 176 (May, 1963), 18.

[40] For the details see R. Leiber, "Pius XII und die Juden in Rom 1943–4," in *Stimmen der Zeit*, 167 (1961), 428–36.

enormity,[41] it is nevertheless the task of the historian to question the validity of such reasons. In the welter of speculation which this issue has raised, it is possible to stress at least two certain points.

The first of these concerns Hitler's own attitude to the Jews. If we were to accept the view that "perhaps never before in history have so many human lives been lost through the passivity of a single politician,"[42] we should have to be convinced that a strong and forceful protest by the Pope would have compelled Hitler to change his mind. Unfortunately, there is not a shred of evidence to support this contention. The extermination of the Jews was in the very forefront of Hitler's plans. It is necessary to remember that his hatred of the Jews long preceded his acquisition of power, and was a goal of equal importance with his dream of Germany's eastward expansion. Tactical considerations were not allowed to modify or alter his plans in any way, for these were the very part and parcel of his inner self, and an integral part of his whole dynamic. The destruction of the Jews added nothing to the successful conduct of the war—indeed it took away scarce resources. Nevertheless, Hitler's plans were carried out with the highest priority and the utmost secrecy. So fanatical was Hitler on this point that he would recognize no objections, however cogent. Even when some rare official raised serious questions about the German occupation policies in Poland, the Ukraine or other occupied areas, it is noteworthy that not a single forcible protest was ever made to Hitler against the extermination of the Jews. These ineluctable facts allow us to draw no comforting speculations about a possibly successful protest on the part of the Pope or anyone else.

Another certainty stems from the nature of the totalitarian regime itself. As Bishop Dibelius pointed out, the only possible basis upon which any opposition could have been organized from within Germany by the Church, was the claim to be defending the legal rights of the Church as recognized in decrees or treaties signed by the totalitarian power itself.[43] For the individual to

[41] Father Leiber stated that the Vatican believed at the time that at least two million people had been exterminated.

[42] Hochhuth, op. cit., p. 285.

[43] Berliner Sonntagsblatt, April 7, 1963.

appeal to the general rights of humanity was useless, for he was immediately silenced by imprisonment or worse. Protests were only possible through the Church leaders, appealing in their turn to the acknowledged position of the Church. A legal complaint did not by any means always succeed—as Ribbentrop acknowledged at Nuremberg, he had received a drawerful of protests from the Papal Nuncio[44]—but it was the only basis which sometimes worked. If the Church leaders seemed to the outside world to be always more interested in trying to defend the interests of the Church itself than in the plight of the Jews, transported laborers, or foreigners, it has to be recognized that only if the integrity of the Church's own position was resolutely defended, could there remain the possibility of any pressure being brought to bear on the totalitarian state. It is therefore necessary to forget the situation as it exists in present-day pluralistic democracies, and to understand the dynamic and overwhelming nature of a totalitarian state such as the Third Reich.

But is that all that can be said? Surely, there will be a continuous raising of the question whether it was not the Pope's responsibility to witness to the truth of the Gospel regardless of the consequences. Did not the whole world look for a clear sign that the representative of Christ would call for the maintenance of Christian ideals, and protest against the violation of Christian morality and the fundamental rights of man? Does not the Church exist to witness to the basic truths of the Christian Gospel, and not to allow these to be overthrown while its leaders remain silent? And did not this silence call in question the whole moral authority of the Church which was acknowledged directly or indirectly by Christian and non-Christian alike? How much worse could matters have been made when already six million Jews had passed to their deaths in the concentration camps, and when violence and terror ruled supreme? Did not appeals for help and comfort come daily to the Vatican? Was not the Pope constantly urged to proclaim the good news of the Gospel to all in adversity, and to protest openly against the wicked sinfulness of the world, even if such a pronouncement could not avert the terrors and calamities of war? After all these years there may be

---

[44] *International Military Tribunal*, X.

now no final certainty about which of the many conflicting motives, pressures, and issues in the end determined the Pope's conduct. But it would be against the evidence not to realize that the issue lay constantly upon the Pope's conscience, whether or not, in the actual reality of the political situation, such a protest would not have caused more evil than good. If he chose to remain silent, it was for reasons of deep conviction, reached through much sorrow and travail of mind. As he wrote to the Bishop of Berlin in 1943: "In constantly striving to find the right balance between the mutually contradictory claims of his pastoral office, the path ahead for the representative of Christ is becoming daily more overgrown, beset with difficulties, and full of thorns."

Patricia Marx Ellsberg
An Interview with Rolf Hochhuth

Rolf Hochhuth was born in Basel, Switzerland, in 1931. He has gained an international reputation for his highly controversial drama, The Deputy, *which was very critical of Pius XII's behavior towards Nazi Germany and the persecution of the Jews. In the play Hochhuth ascribed these actions to weaknesses in the personal character of Eugenio Pacelli (Pius XII) and even to utilitarian motives.*

In February 1964, shortly after his play came out, Hochhuth visited the United States. He was interviewed at that time by Patricia Marx over WNYC, the city-operated radio station of New York. The translation of Mr. Hochhuth's answers was prepared by John Simon, who served as interpreter of the broadcast. At the time of this interview Professor Conway's article in defense of Pius XII had not been published. Does it seem likely that Hochhuth would have significantly modified his contentions if he had had an opportunity to read Conway?

SOURCE. Patricia Marx, "Interview with Rolf Hochhuth," © 1964 *Partisan Review,* XXXI, No. 3 (Summer, 1964) , pp. 363–376. By kind permission of the *Partisan Review.*

Marx. Mr. Hochhuth, *The Deputy* is your first play to be published. Had you been thinking of writing a drama before you became interested in this subject?

Hochhuth. No, I had not started a play before *The Deputy;* and, before that, I wrote non-dramatic prose.

Marx. Why did you decide to treat such a vast historical subject in the form of a play?

Hochhuth. Because I believe that this subject is, in itself, such that a play is the appropriate form, especially when you consider that the argument of the play hardly had to be invented by me, but could be taken directly from actual events—I mean, Gerstein bursting in upon the Papal Nuncio. I believe that in a play historical events can be marshalled toward the dramatic climax, and different points of view can be made to clash more sharply, and forcefully, than in a work of fiction.

Also, I felt challenged by the notion of writing a play in free verse—something that had been ignored in German literature for some forty years; to be precise, since *Der Rosenkavalier* and other works by Hofmannsthal. Whereas, in England and America, it was common practice; Christopher Fry and T. S. Eliot are instances. And I was particularly influenced by Auden's *The Age of Anxiety.*

Marx. Why did you use free verse rather than prose?

Hochhuth. That, too, hinges on the choice of the dramatic form. Free verse carries its speaker along much more readily than prose, especially when it concerns a subject which is so closely involved with contemporary events and depends so extensively on historical documents. Then, things must be transposed, heightened by language. Otherwise it would often sound as if one were merely quoting from the documents.

Of course, the choice of a heightened language—whether we convey it through free verse, or however—was made easier for me by the milieu of the play. Anyone who talks, for example, to high church dignitaries, will find that they do not speak in an ordinary, everyday language, but that they express themselves, as a matter of course, in a more ceremonial manner—as it were, words on cothurni. I do not think, however, that it is still possible to write a drama in classical verse form, when the characters are people from our walk of life.

Marx. Mr. Hochhuth, did you feel constrained, as an artist, to be historically accurate? Was there a conflict between you as an artist, and you as an historian?

Hochhuth. Only inasmuch as writing a play about events that lie only two decades behind us required a much more intensive research into historical documents than if one were writing, say, a play about Luther.

Marx. How did the idea for the play present itself? How did it take shape?

Hochhuth. It all happened a long time ago, and it is very hard for me to reconstruct exactly how it began. I think I took down a few notes, referring to the character of Gerstein, because my idea was to write a short story about him—quite a long time ago.

Later, however, in 1956, I met a man in Austria who had helped with the gassing in Auschwitz. He had been transferred there as political punishment. And I read accounts which referred back to this subject. Then it first became clear to me what the form of the play must be.

Also, at that time, the book, *The Third Reich and the Jews*, which contained the report of Gerstein, was published. And then, in 1958, a book appeared containing the documents concerning the Vatican's attitude toward the deportation of Jews from Rome. At that time, I was living in Münster because my wife was a student there; and I heard accounts of a vain attempt to arrest Bishop Galen—or rather, of the Nazis' hesitation to imprison him. I cannot say more than this. It is now seven years ago. It all fitted itself together like a mosaic.

Then, the actual work on the play began—my daily work on it starting in the spring of 1959.

Marx. How did the Pope enter into the play?

Hochhuth. That came about with the consideration—with the question of how, in this so-called Christian Europe, the murder of an entire people could take place without the highest moral authority of this earth having a word to say about it.

Marx. In the beginning, then, the Pope wasn't in the play at all?

Hochhuth. Well, there had appeared, as I said, some documents about the attitude of the Vatican, which have a voice in the play. But it all developed in such a way that the most meaningful antagonist of Riccardo could be none other than the highest moral authority—precisely because he makes a demand which only this highest moral authority can meet.

Marx. Mr. Hochhuth, what writers influenced you the most?

Hochhuth. Dramatists did not influence me so much as novelists, or letter-writers.

I am always being asked, for example, why I did not study Brecht. When I started writing, I was so much under the influence of Thomas Mann that everything I wrote painfully echoed this great man. As a beginner, one simply cannot resist him; indeed, there is a very well known German writer who today, in his sixties, is still so much under the spell of Thomas Mann that he has practically no independence, which was very much my case, too. That is why I wanted to prevent, at all costs, something like this happening to me with Brecht, and I went out of my way to ignore him.

Naturally, I read many classical plays: the ancients, and Shakespeare, and also the Germans, including Hauptmann. But my concept of life in the perspective of history was influenced much more by novelists and story-tellers and above all, by the great German historians—by Mommsen, very decisively.

I read him, not for his subject matter, which of course is Roman history, but simply because man's bearing, his historic stance, can most readily be deciphered through the study of history. This, for me, is, and will surely remain, the most interesting area of investigation. I shall never forget (though it does not strictly bear on this) a sentence in Mommsen that really sank in, that I'll probably always carry with me. It concerns an invasion of Sicily. Mommsen writes, with icily laconic concentration: "The men were killed; their women and children distributed among the soldiery." You see, I find that such sentences contain all of history; and, when such insights are later combined with the experiences one has had in one's own time—during the aerial bombardments or just altogether during the Third Reich—then one realizes that history is man's great fatality, and, God knows, a great field of study for the man of letters.

Marx. Many critics feel that your work has greater historical and moral value than artistic value. I wonder what your response is to that evaluation of your play?

Hochhuth. That is a question of who is doing the criticizing. The historians, with few exceptions, find it interesting as literature—and the *literati* find it historically interesting. I cannot defend myself against this, and can only hope that time will sort it all out—and, in any case, I will not allow myself to be deterred from writing about what I find interesting, even if my next play should again be a historical one.

I think that literary criticism, in some measure, was thrown into mild consternation by the fact that someone had, again, written historical drama. None had been written—not for decades, I mean. Brecht's *Galileo* isn't, in the sense I mean, a historical play. But the simple fact that the writing of historical plays is no longer practiced does not mean that one shouldn't try one's hand at it all the same.

It is scarcely conceivable why, for example, a marital drama should be more interesting than a play which deals with, let us say, the extermination of the Albigensians. With this prerequisite, however: a historic drama today, I believe, is legitimate only when the author makes use of history merely as a blueprint from which to construct the behavior of man in our time. When he is, in other words, not merely giving a picture of the times, a giant fresco of the past, but is concerned with something indicative, with characters who behave in a way significant of our actions and feelings. The condescension with which a few—and it was only a few—men of letters tried to dismiss me as a mere historiographer, especially funny because it is particularly in the realm of literature that I conquered new ground, at least in Germany, by writing the first verse play we have these days.

I am highly sceptical of the fuss which is made about novels, novels that have no bearing on reality and that are each time celebrated as a great event for some four weeks by twenty-two people.

I must tell you that when I recently saw Ingmar Bergman's *The Silence,* I left that Hamburg movie house with the question, "What is there left for the novelist today?" Think of what Bergman can do with a single shot of his camera, up a street, down a corridor, into a woman's armpit. Of all he can say without saying a single word. The entire film consists perhaps of three pages of typescript. What then can a novelist offer of comparable interest with mere words?

Marx. Mr. Hochhuth, how does this relate to the drama? Is it the same thing to some degree?

Hochhuth. I don't think that the drama faces the same problem. Film has this more pronouncedly epic, narrative character, whereas drama is tied to theses, to the conflict of ideas. These are things that a film cannot tackle in its non-verbal way, such as the confronting of arguments with counter-arguments. The drama cannot dispense with words. In film, the narrative element may well be bound up much more with the image that can be conjured up without words, if one only knows how to command one's camera.

Marx. Are you thinking of writing a film yourself?

Hochhuth. Never. I lack the technical orientation and know-how. But if something I have written lends itself to being adapted to the film, all good and well as far as I'm concerned.

Marx. What did you mean earlier, Mr. Hochhuth, when you referred to history as fatality?

Hochhuth. I'm influenced in this by various writers, like Theodor Lessing, the author of *History as Rationale of the Irrational.* Theodor Lessing's very life was depressing proof of the rightness of his thesis. In 1933, he was shot to death by the Nazis as he sat in his study.

Even as a boy of thirteen I felt history in a very blunt, subconscious, sub-intellectual way, as a fatality that has sway over us and against which we can defend ourselves only very partially.

Marx. To what degree is man responsible for his own fate or his own actions, then?

Hochhuth. I have just been involved in a heated debate with a German periodical which accused me of being so very primitive in my thinking as still to maintain that it is great men who make history. And that I have not been aware of the fact that this is not so. But the periodical did not say who, then, does make history; and I am very much of the opinion that the history of World War II would have looked very different if Hitler and Churchill had never been born. And indeed I would subscribe to the notion that it would be the end of the drama if one were to take the position that man cannot be held responsible for his fate.

At the end of my "Historical Sidelights," I quote Melchinger. "But if the individual can no longer be held responsible, either because he is no longer in a position to decide or else does not understand that he must decide, then we have an alibi for all guilt. And that would mean the end of drama. For 'there can be no suspense without freedom of decision in each given case.' "

Marx. How can this be reconciled with the idea of history as fatality, then?

Hochhuth. This contradiction *is* the fatality. Man is meant to act, to be responsible. He should be the master of his fate. He should be moral, and history continually brings him into conflict with powers which condemn him to defeat, which are stronger than he and which destroy him. I am thoroughly of the opinion that this is an area which should be of interest even to the gentlemen of literature. Consider merely one very fruitful example: obligatory military conscription in this twentieth century. Compulsory military service is an invention of the French Revolution as much as is the secret police and has completely changed the lives of people.

Consider only what irresoluble conflicts arise from the fact that as one completes his eighteenth year, he is simply forced to put on a uniform and start shooting.

Marx. But if you're being attacked by an enemy, isn't it necessary that you defend your country?

Hochhuth. Absolutely. I am not a pacifist at all because I'm of the opinion that it is irresponsible to allow oneself to be driven into traps. Imagine simply what would have happened if the Russians in 1941 had not defended themselves against the Nazis. What would have become of the Russian people? However, for the Russian soldier this did not produce a tragic situation, or hardly. He was fighting for his country. A tragic situation occurred for any particular Russian soldier, who was a passionate anti-Communist and who none the less had to fight with the Communist army against the invaders, for the benefit of Communism just as much as for the benefit of his country. This same kind of tragic situation occurred, of course, for many Germans, who could not possibly have wished that Hitler should triumph but who no more wished that the Russians should march all the way to the Rhine. Indeed there is no human conflict possible, conflict, let us say, in marriage or in love or anywhere else, which does not get its most fundamental intensification in the context of history.

Marx. In the context of history as fatality, how would you define the Pope's guilt or responsibility in terms of not protesting against the slaughter of the Jews?

Hochhuth. That is a question whose answer cannot possibly be reduced to a simple formula. So very many things have contributed to the Pope's behaving as he, unfortunately, did. Looking at it purely from the outside, one can say, for instance, that fatality began with the fact that on the very eve of the Second World War Pope Pius XI, who was a very brave and very resolute man, should have died. Furthermore, again looking from the outside, it may have been only a coincidence, but then again perhaps truly fatality, that his successor should have been a Pope who in his perfectly legitimate predilection for everything German, for the German people, overlooked the fact that the Nazis were not "The Germans" but the despoilers, the perverters of Germany, as well as of everything else.

Marx. Granting the fact that the Nazis might have retaliated, do you feel that the Pope should have protested anyway?

Hochhuth. Absolutely. And I would say this not merely off the top of my head but out of the very reasons which Riccardo cites in his conversation with his father in the second act of my play. This is emphatically substantiated in the play, always presupposing that one takes the office of the Pope seriously, and that one is really ready to measure this man by his own pretensions, which are of course enormous.

Marx. Was the Pope then under a different kind of moral obligation toward his fellow man than a man of another faith?

Hochhuth. Well, the Catholic Church lays claim to being the only church that bestows salvation. It should naturally devolve on it to feel responsible for all human beings, all religions, all races. This is all the more so—though many Catholic priests deny it—because Pius XII had without doubt no anti-Semitic feelings. You might be interested, if we have a little time, in hearing an anecdote which was actually the most terrifying experience I had since the publication of my play.

I received a visit one day from a very intelligent, older, and quite well-known Jesuit priest, who spent an entire Sunday with my wife and me, chatting. What this man said so enormously frightened me that twice I countered him with a quotation which stands at the very beginning of my play, and comes from Bernard Shaw, "Beware of the man whose God is in Heaven." This Jesuit father spoke to me as follows: "If humanism were right, but humanism is only a fashion, then you too would be right in your play. For man is not really the measure of all things. Antiquity is wrong when it asserts that man is the measure of all things." And he went on, literally: "Man is excrement, at least in the aspect of eternity."

And that, presumably, is to this day—much more than she admits it—the view of the Church. The Jesuit went on, "Certainly it is frightful, what was done to the Jews and to the 56 million people of all faiths who were devoured by the Second World War, but then again it is not *so* frightful, because all of them are with God, not one of them was lost. They are all preserved. No soul is lost, not even that of Hitler or of Himmler. Before God this will all someday become unsubstantial and forgiven." And he went on, "The Bible has an example ready which really cuts the ground out from under *The Deputy*." And he said, "Jesus did not lift a finger to have St. John the Baptist rescued from Herod's prison, for obviously Jesus must have felt that this man had fulfilled his mission on earth." I, on the other hand, not being conversant with the historical circumstances of that particular time, asked: "Father, was Jesus in a position to do something about that in the first place?"

The Jesuit could not answer my question precisely, but he said that he believed Jesus could have acted because he already had the people very much on his side. I said to him then, because his tremendous hardness impressed me, "Father, I am ready to believe that you would not bat an eyelash if you were informed that in ten minutes you would be beheaded." He smiled at that. He liked that. I then continued, "I also believe that you would not bat an eyelash if you were in the cell of a human being who, five minutes later, would be executed." And on this Sunday I became cognizant for the first time of what bottomless cunning lurks in the Church's insistence on celibacy. That these priests are obliged to live alone, that they do not have a single human being to whom they can get thoroughly attached. They have no child, no wife, and this gives them that unbelievable hardness, which enables them to reckon years, not in the terms of a human life, but incommensurably under the aspect of eternity. They are not permitted to live. They are not permitted to have a life of their own, and therefore life itself, the life of other people, is not of the same consequence to them as life is for those to whom that is all there is.

And it is from this position—I am now completely clear about this—that the Church was able, from the beginning, to draw the strength to demand for 2,000 years such unheard of sacrifices and victims. This brutality is true of all great promulgators of ideas. So, too, the Nazis were willing to sacrifice one half of the German people in the Second World War because they felt they were building an empire, a kingdom of a thousand years. The Bolshevists, too, reckon not in our measures of time but in terms of centuries. They do not think of the happiness of the living but in terms of generations and generations to come—that eventually things will become better. But it is always terribly inhuman to think in this way.

Marx. Mr. Hochhuth, your characterization of the Pope emphasizes his concern for earthly things, such as factories and the political realities of Europe vs. Russia. Were you at that time unaware of his transcendental view of life?

Hochhuth. Well, first of all, I must say that in no part of my play did I submit that the financial concerns of the Vatican caused the silence of the Pope. That I did not maintain anywhere. I put the scene dealing with finances before the actual drama concerning the deportation of the Jews from Rome because I'm thoroughly of the opinion that the Vatican does indeed have very substantial earthly interests, but I do not reproach it with that. I must, however, add that this conversation with the Jesuit did not occur until after the appearance of my play, and that today it seems very good for me that this conversation occurred as late as it did. I am now firmly convinced that this calculation in terms of eons, of gigantic chunks of time, played its part in the Pope's decision. But even today I would hardly dare to represent the Pope with this kind of metaphysical hardness. Let us hope that he was really concerned with the political and historical arguments, the charitable arguments, which are proposed in the fourth act as his motivation, and that it was these arguments alone which brought him to this awful decision. If it were otherwise, then the decision and indeed the Church itself would have to be conceived of as altógether inimical to life. I found this attitude of the Jesuit extremely inimical to life and indeed I told him so. But this did not concern him very much, for life is, for him, not the first and last consideration, whereas to us ordinary mortals who are not firmly embedded in our faith—and who is nowadays?—to us, life is very much the first and last concern.

That Pius XII himself, of course, was influenced by this kind of ecclesiastic thinking or that he embodied it himself to a very large degree is proven in any case by a speech which I transcribed and included in my fourth act. A speech he made about the Poles when, in their need and despair, they asked him for help:

"As the flowers of the countryside wait beneath winter's mantle of snow for the warm breezes of spring, so the Jews must wait, praying and trusting that the hour of heavenly comfort will come."

I didn't change anything in this except one single word. Instead of the word "Poles" I used the word "Jews." That is the whole story.

Marx. Mr. Hochhuth, is a religious faith in another world inimical to the kind of humanism that you value? Is it a necessary consequence of this belief that human life is not taken seriously on this earth?

Hochhuth. For God's sake, no. Faith is a good thing, and I envy any human being who is firmly established in it. But he must not, or he should not, be led by his faith into any kind of neglect of the matters of this earth. Obviously our turn will come, the turn of all of us, someday; and probably everyone has at least for a moment of every day, the feeling of resignation toward the things of this earth. A moment when he knows that to founder here below is the ultimate, that which is destined for all of us, no matter how great our earthly involvement, no matter how great our ambition. Then it is very good to have faith. Then it is probably the sole salvation to have faith. But as long as we have the courage or the brutality to bring children into this world, a world which, for example, has an atom bomb in it, for that long we must not reckon in terms of eternity, and, out of regard for eternity, neglect our earthly involvements.

Marx. Mr. Hochhuth, would you care to define or describe your own religious views?

Hochhuth. At the utmost, I can quote a saying of Bismarck's, which has perhaps been made use of all too little, even though it should be of help to the intellectuals.

A friend once asked Bismarck how he had overcome the radical nihilism of his youth. He said, "I recalled the advance patrols of my doubts, which had ventured too far forward, with all firmness." In other words, an act of the will, and probably that is the only way it can be done. One cannot wait for grace to bestow faith upon one.

Marx. Do you mean that it's a matter of will to quell doubts and to accept a faith?

Hochhuth. I think that absolutely, that it is an act of the will, because, after all, we are daily attacked by doubts and could not live if we did not chase them back into the corner.

Marx. Is there any principle that guides you in regard to what things you will choose to believe in?

Hochhuth. I don't believe so, but I haven't thought enough about it. I think that the personal experiences of every individual life, which will be different from one person to another, must be the determining factor.

Marx. Mr. Hochhuth, you were only fourteen at the end of the war. How do you feel that you would have behaved if you had been a responsible adult during the war?

Hochhuth. I would have behaved just as well or as badly as all other contemporaries. I am sure that I would not have been a particularly brave fellow. I think it also depends on whether one has a family or not. I find that there are many excuses, very legitimate excuses, for fathers of families, who know that they have children, that they have a wife, who will be killed if they, the men, dare go too far. That should not be overlooked by us today.

Marx. Mr. Hochhuth, were the actions of Riccardo, the central figure of the play, the ones that you respect the most? Was his behavior, leading to his martyrdom, the only right way to act?

Hochhuth. For artistic reasons I tried of course, to make Riccardo a living human being, with all the contradictions that entails. He was not to become a mere moral trumpeter, but a human being who makes mistakes, who goes too far, who overshoots the mark, who, for instance, considers Hitler's chances in Russia much better than they actually were, which was exactly what his contemporaries did at the time. Or if you think of that central passage in the drama, Riccardo's foolhardy decision to do away with the Pope and to make the SS take the rap for the murder, in order to mobilize the world's indignation against them. This scene, to be sure, is not intended realistically at all. It is merely a vehicle for pushing theoretical thought to its extreme limits. This is why I cannot answer your question with an unqualified yes. But the essential concern of Riccardo, the moral impetus which propels him, and his coming out strongly for the victims—this I find indeed to be essentially what one should have expected of the priests in such a situation, and what many of them, more than a thousand, actually did.

Marx. Would you expect this from a man who is not a Catholic?

Hochhuth. It cannot be expected or demanded of anyone. One cannot even demand it of a priest. The determination to become a martyr is a very personal decision which not even the Pope can demand of his priests. But this is why I laid the scene of the deportation of the Jews in Rome, the Pope's own diocese, where the Pope was personally, as an individual, as Eugene Pacelli, confronted with this problem and able to make a personal decision.

Marx. If you can't demand martyrdom, where do you place limits on what you can expect of a moral human being?

Hochhuth. That is a very important question. You yourself said before that I established in great detail all the diplomatic opportunities of the Vatican toward the co-signatory of the Concordat, Hitler. Opportunities which would not have placed the Church in danger, but which could nonetheless have been exploited to resist Hitler. These should have been fully exploited: anything that within the realm of diplomacy could have been mustered up by way of threats against Hitler. But beyond that I would say that the Pope also had the duty to obligate the countless Catholics in the East—in Poland, in Hungary, for example, and also certainly the Catholics in Germany—to obligate them not to participate in mass murder. It is inconceivable how many people could have been saved just in Poland if the population had been summoned by the Church to offer Jews a hiding place.

Marx. So short of martyrdom or risking the lives of Catholics, you feel that it was incumbent upon the Pope and the Church to do what they could for the welfare of the Jews.

Hochhuth. Of course.

Marx. Mr. Hochhuth, several times in the play you mention that characters in the play now hold responsible positions in Germany. Does the possibility of a resurgence of Nazism disturb you?

Hochhuth. I wasn't thinking of any particular persons. I was inventing my personages freely, except, of course, for those who are historical figures. I consider it completely out of the question that a new wave of National Socialism is to be feared in Germany. The Germans have been burnt, and a burnt child fears the fire. I think they are cured for this century. What our greatgrandchildren will do, we do not know. But I do not believe that, in view of the bad odor National Socialism has acquired, the neighbors of a new Hitler would permit him to come to power in the first place. Let us hope not, anyway.

However, there's an exception which we must mention here. There are those as yet underdeveloped countries which have just acquired their independence, like Egypt, in which nationalism is, at the moment, bearing terrible fruits.

Marx. Mr. Hochhuth, you have called this an age of fence-sitters. Who do you feel is guilty of fence-sitting now, and about what things are we not committing ourselves that we should take stands on?

Hochhuth. I meant that somewhat differently. I said that I consider it fatal if we allow ourselves to be influenced by the chitchat of the editorial writers about our living in an age of the masses, which, naturally, is true to some extent. But we must not allow this to induce a person to think only of his impotence, and not of the fact that as an individual he must always bear the responsibility not only for his family but for the entire community.

One must breed a sense of responsibility. It must begin at school. This naturally presupposes that even the intellectuals should clearly realize that even the least significant salesgirl who was born, perhaps, in a tenement, and who never reads a book and never goes to the theatre, is a human being like ourselves and that her face is to be respected just as much, do you understand, as our own. And that we ourselves, if we must speak about the masses, have to be quite conscious of our belonging to these masses just as much as that salesgirl. Even as we wish to be respected as individual within the mass, and so respect ourselves, we must see the individual equally in every other person whatever his class. I believe that that is a good working principle for the inculcation of individual responsibility.

Marx. What do you feel is the most effective way of teaching this sense of responsibility?

Hochhuth. I am not a pedagogue, but to reduce it to a formula, man should be taught to see in every one of his fellows, be he ever so fleabitten and personally distasteful, a creature to be respected as an individual, as a creature of God, just like oneself.

Marx. Are there any other themes or subjects about which you feel you could write as forceful and dramatic a play as *The Deputy?*

Hochhuth. Oh, yes. But by this I do not wish to imply that I will again be lucky enough to write as good a play, if I have written a good play at all. But themes of this sort exist, alas, in multitudes.

Marx. What would these themes be, for instance?

Hochhuth. Well, take for example that appalling fact which began to establish itself in European history once since the 'twenties, but which has since then established itself ever more firmly. In the First World War, as far as I know, it was still an unthinkable thing that both warring factions should, without so much as stopping to think, implicate individuals, civilians, in the military action. No soldier then who had any sense of honor in him would have shot without hesitation at women and children. The Second World War, and previous to that, the Spanish Civil War, (just think of Picasso's picture, "Guernica") were to institute it as a matter of most idiotic fact for both sides to wage war quite naturally against open cities. This might be a good subject for a play: to what extent is a soldier obligated to refuse the command to kill civilians?

Now you might be of the opinion that this is a banal question, a platitude. But I believe that the topics which are of the greatest concern to all of us are always these very banalities, subject matters which are, as it were, lying around in the street, waiting to be picked up. The subject matter of *The Deputy* was also lying in the street. I would be inclined to say that it could become an artistic program to pick up those topics off the streets.

Marx. Mr. Hochhuth, what is your artistic program for the future?

Hochhuth. I would like to write a play and then three or four short stories, if I can.

Marx. Do you already have a subject for the play?

Hochhuth. Yes, certainly, but it is as yet a little too complicated to speak about it, and above all things, it would be premature because I am still working on the plot outline and am not quite certain about the direction in which things will develop. It isn't as if one were in full command of one's material beforehand. To begin with the material commands the writer. One must find a way of grasping and shaping it.

Marx. Mr. Hochhuth, before *The Deputy* was published and performed you were not a particularly well-known figure in Germany. What effect has fame had on you personally?

Hochhuth. I was completely unknown. I edited books, as thousands of other people do. Editions of the classics. But otherwise I was totally unheard of.

Marx. How did this sudden attention affect you?

Hochhuth. It frightened me, but it also had its good side, I hope. It brought me many friends—not my reputation, but my book. Many friends whom I otherwise would never have met and who now enrich my life. I might add, of course, that such great repercussions stemming from one's first play place a considerable mortgage on one's next play, even before it is written.

And it is my great concern, which preoccupies me day and night, whether with my new play, or with any new literary work, I will be able to fulfill what is now expected of me.

Marx. Mr. Hochhuth, I want to thank you very much for this interview.

Hochhuth. I want to thank you. It was a truly pleasant afternoon, and I really had a good time, although I would not have thought it possible that I could still enjoy talking about my play. Thank you.

PART THREE

The Papacy and the Second World War

Saul A. Friedlaender
Pius XII and the German Invasion of
The Low Countries

The author of this selection is a Swiss scholar. His annotated collection of documents first appeared in a French edition in 1964. Some critics have observed that his choice of documents is partial. His main sources have been the records of the German Foreign Ministry, particularly the files of its Vatican embassy, which was maintained until 1945. Friedlaender did not make use of documents that have been published by the Vatican archives, nor did he utilize the documents of the German Foreign Ministry that were mimeographed in the NG series at the Nuremberg trials and provided some evidence of representations made by the Papal Nuncio in Berlin against the persecution of the Church by the Nazis.

In contrast to the writers who have commented favorably on Pius XII's messages of sympathy to the rulers of Belgium, the Netherlands, and Luxembourg when those countries were invaded by Hitler's armies on May 10, 1940, Dr. Friedlaender asks why did not Pius also speak out when Protestant Norway and Denmark were invaded a few weeks before? Could it be that Pius was moved only when the fate of substantial numbers of Roman Catholics was involved?

SOURCE. From Saul A. Friedlaender, *Pius XII and the Third Reich: A Documentation* (translated from the French and German by Charles Fullman; New York: Alfred A. Knopf, 1966), pp. 48–53. By kind permission of Alfred A. Knopf, New York, and Chatto & Windus, Ltd. (Laurence Pollinger, Ltd.), London. Footnotes renumbered.

The Invasion of Belgium, Holland, and Luxembourg

On May 10, Belgium, Holland, and Luxembourg were invaded, and the Pope abandoned his reserve. That same day, he addressed a message to the sovereigns of the three countries that had been attacked.

To King Leopold, the Sovereign Pontiff wrote:

"At this moment when the Belgian people, against their will and contrary to their right, see their territory exposed for the second time to the cruelties of war, We are profoundly moved, and We send to Your Majesty and all your well-beloved nation the assurance of Our paternal affection; and as We pray to Almighty God that this sore trial may end with the restoration of Belgium's full liberty and independence, We bestow upon Your Majesty and his people, with all Our heart, Our apostolic blessing."

To Queen Wilhelmina:

"Having learned with intense emotion that Your Majesty's efforts for peace have not succeeded in preserving a noble people from becoming involved in a theater of war, We beseech God, the Supreme Arbiter of the destinies of nations, to hasten by His almighty aid the restoration of peace and liberty."[1]

On May 11, Bergen wired to Berlin:

"From a source well informed about Pope's intentions, I hear that Pope's telegrams to King of the Belgians, Queen of the Netherlands and Grand Duchess of Luxembourg, published this evening in *L'Osservatore Romano,* are not to be construed as political intervention, let alone unilateral condemnation of German action. Pronouncements contained no word of protest. Pope had merely intended to express to the heads of state and peoples concerned his sorrow at the fact that they were being drawn into

---

[1] Paul Duclos: *Le Vatican et la Seconde Guerre Mondiale* (Paris: Pedone; 1955), p. 59.

the conflict against their will and were being directly affected by the hardships of war.

"Message to the King of the Belgians is not a reply to his appeal to Pius XII making one-sided charges against Germany, but crossed it."[2]

Next day, Ambassador Dino Alfieri was instructed to protest to the Pope in the name of the Duce. Hans Georg von Mackensen, the Ambassador of the Reich at the Quirinal, reported what the Italian diplomat had told him of his talk with Pius XII:

"Alfieri told me very confidentially during farewell visit today that in the course of his farewell audience with the Pope he told the latter in serious terms, on the Duce's instructions, that Pope's telegrams to Belgium and Holland had had a very painful effect on the Duce. Pope countered that in the telegrams, which were the result of hours of reflection, he had spoken only as the Supreme Pontiff standing aloof from all mundane happenings and had scrupulously avoided any word of political import, such as 'invasion,' that might imply a viewpoint. Alfieri said he had replied that such a separation between the priesthood and politics was impossible, because the mere fact that the telegrams were sent was a political act. Moreover, he said, the Pope must not forget that there were 30 million Catholics living in the Reich. The interview, Alfieri thought, had been 'very tough.' "[3]

Some days later, Alfieri arrived in Berlin to become the new Italian Ambassador. During his first visit to Woermann, he reported details of his interview with the Pope; his account tallied in the main with the details he had already supplied to Mackensen, but he added one important point:

"The Pope, he said, had been astonished that there were objections to the attitude of *L'Osservatore Romano* and had promised to give instructions again that this journal was not to take sides clearly in favor of Britain and France . . ."

Then the Ambassador added:

". . . that both Germany and Italy had an interest in being on

[2] Telegram from Bergen to Berlin, May 11, 1940, StS: V, AA, Bonn (MS).
[3] Telegram from Mackensen to Berlin, May 13, 1940; ibid. (MS).

good terms with the Vatican, at least for the duration of the War. What would come afterwards remained to be seen."[4]

Finally, Alfieri related his conversation with the Pope in his memoirs, adding a detail often quoted since:

"The duties inherent in my office made it necessary to express, in accordance with instructions received from Ciano, the Duce's regret at the prominence which the Catholic newspapers, and in particular *L'Osservatore Romano,* had given to the three telegrams sent by the Holy Father to the King of the Belgians, the Queen of Holland, and the Grand Duchess of Luxembourg following 'the unjust invasion of their territories by Nazi troops.'

"The Holy Father replied that he found the Duce's irritation incomprehensible . . . 'Whatever happens in the future,' concluded the Holy Father calmly but firmly, 'even if they come and take me off to a concentration camp, I have absolutely nothing with which to reproach myself. Every man will be answerable to God for his own actions.' "[5]

The first thought that impresses itself on the mind as one reads these texts is the same as that which could have been prompted by the encyclical *Summi Pontificatus.* The Pope, who had been moved to express his pain at the sufferings of Poland, this time voiced his emotions to the Belgians, the Dutch, and the Luxembourgers. Why would he keep silent when there were Jews involved? Perhaps, at this stage, we may suggest the first ingredient of an answer which will doubtless contain other, more important elements. This part of the answer is supplied to us by an article in *L'Osservatore Romano,* published a few weeks before the German attack in Flanders and immediately after the aggression of the Reich against Denmark and Norway, two small, neutral states. The Pope refrained from any reaction. Yet, was not the situation similar to that which arose out of the attack on Belgium, Holland, and Luxembourg? *L'Osservatore Romano* enables us to grasp the difference when, in an article attempting to

[4] Memorandum by Woermann, May 19, 1940, *DGFP* (D, IX) , p. 378.
[5] Dino Alfieri: *Dictators Face to Face* (New York: New York University Press; 1955) , pp. 16 f.

justify the silence of the Sovereign Pontiff in the face of the events in Scandinavia, the organ of the Vatican writes:

"There are only 2,000 Catholics in Norway; that being so, the Holy See, though severely condemning the moral aspect of the matter, must take a practical view and bear in mind the 30 million German Catholics."[6]

Now, in Belgium the population is predominantly Catholic; there are also numerous Catholics in Holland and Luxembourg; the same is true of Poland. Though one hesitates to draw a conclusion, one cannot entirely dismiss the question: Did not the Sovereign Pontiff openly condemn violence and aggression only when the victims were Catholics? This hypothesis is not tendentious. It simply implies that the Pope conceived his duty within very narrow limits.

Moreover, the Sovereign Pontiff's caution grew more marked, keeping pace with the rhythm of the German victories. On May 18, Bergen supplied new data on the interpretation which the Vatican henceforth would place on the three telegrams:

". . . was intimated at the office of the Secretary of State that Pope, foreseeing King Leopold's telegram, wanted to anticipate it and avoid answering. In this connection, it was emphasized that telegrams were not intended as any kind of barb against Germany."[7]

The Vatican radio emphasized on May 21, in an English-language broadcast,[8] that in his messages and words the Pope had always deliberately refrained from showing any particular sympathy for, or adopting an attitude toward, one of the belligerents.[9] On May 16, *L'Osservatore Romano* had terminated its political commentaries.[10]

---

[6] Duclos: *op. cit.*, pp. 58 f.

[7] Telegram from Bergen to Berlin, May 18, 1940, StS: V, AA, Bonn (MS).

[8] It has not been possible to find any reference to that broadcast cited by Bergen.

[9] Telegram from Bergen to Berlin, May 22, 1940, ibid. (MS).

[10] Duclos: *op. cit.*, p. 61.

Harold C. Deutsch
The Vatican Exchanges of 1939–1940

Harold C. Deutsch (1904–   ) is a professor of European history at the University of Minnesota. He served as chief of the research and analysis branch of the Office of Strategic Services in Paris and Germany in 1944–1945 and was a member of the U.S. State Department's Special Interrogation Mission in 1945.

In this excerpt from The Conspiracy against Hitler in the Twilight War, *Deutsch reviews highlights of the Vatican's role as intermediary between Britain and the German anti-Nazi plotters from September 1939 to May 1940. The role of Pius XII in this conspiracy had been known in a general way since 1946, but Deutsch's book is the first intensive study of it. His account is based on testimony of over 50 witnesses—virtually all the participants or observers who survived the period. The author's central sources were two participants who were at the core of the affair: Josef Mueller, the Opposition agent who dealt with the Pope and who later became the Bavarian Minister of Justice, and the Rev. Robert Leiber, S.J., the pope's confidential aide.*

How does Professor Deutsch's evaluation of Pius XII's general attitude and his specific messages to the rulers of the Low Countries differ from that of Friedlaender?

The Vatican Exchanges Reviewed

Such, then, is the story of the Vatican exchanges of 1939–40 and their more immediate sequelae. Pius XII is shown in a light that finds little reflection elsewhere in the history of his pontificate. He gambled this once and lost. But the risk, however great for the Church and himself, was incurred for the greatest stake

SOURCE. From Harold C. Deutsch, *The Conspiracy Against Hitler in the Twilight War*, pp. 349–352, University of Minnesota Press, Minneapolis. Copyright © 1968 University of Minnesota.

of all—world peace. As a high British official said to Father Leiber after the Allies entered Rome in 1944: "Pius XII in his efforts for peace went to the outer limits of what was possible for a
Pope."[1]

This Pontiff was by nature reserved and even somewhat timid.
When at all possible, he took the most conciliatory position, as in
his remarks to the German ambassador on New Year's Day,
1940.[2] A mere reading of the documents of his pontificate, of
which he destroyed all the more personal ones, will often fail to
do justice to the firmness of which he was capable in dealing
with some of the problems that arose in the Holy See's relations
with the Third Reich. Least of all do they reflect his personal
sentiments. The degree to which his feelings could be engaged is
illustrated by his remarks to Leiber when he agreed to undertake
the role of intermediary, and especially by the secret steps he
took to warn the Low Countries and the public ones which followed on May 10. When early in the morning he received the
fell tidings of their invasion, he immediately ordered the preparation of a protest against the Nazi aggression toward the neutral
states. Cardinal Maglione accordingly prepared a brief statement
which he proposed to publish over his own signature in *Osservatore Romano* that evening. This Pius straightway rejected as inadequate for the circumstances, a view he reiterated when Maglione next submitted a draft of a letter which the Pope would
address to him and which was also intended for the Vatican journal.
It was then eight o'clock in the evening and a decision had become
pressing. The Pope thereupon determined on the more direct
step of addressing messages of sympathy to the three Low-
lands sovereigns. These he wrote out personally on his little type-
writer and corrected in his own hand. Because of the late hour
he did not wait to get Maglione's counter-signatures but added
them himself.[3]

---

[1] Leiber, in *Stimmen der Zeit*, Vol. 163, p. 99.

[2] Saul Friedländer, *Pius XII and the Third Reich: A Documentation*
(New York, 1966), pp. 40–41.

[3] For the text of the proposed statements of Maglione and the Pope in
Osservatore Romano and the three telegrams see Tardini, pp. 116–119. More
recently they have been published in *Le Saint Siège et la guerre en Europe*,
pp. 444–447.

Each of the three messages contained not only expressions of sympathy but words whose import was condemnation of the cruel and unjust deed of the invader. Whether spurred on by Berlin or not, Mussolini undertook, on May 13, an effort at intimidation. In an audience of leave-taking given the Italian envoy, Dino Alfieri, who was exchanging his post at the Vatican for one in Berlin, the conversation took on a particularly grave tone. The ambassador stated that the Duce found in the three telegrams "a cause of lively displeasure," regarding them "a gesture against his policy." Alfieri then pointed to tension and agitation in Fascist quarters which "did not even exclude something serious happening." In response to this bare threat of mob violence against the Holy See, Pius observed serenely that he was not afraid of a concentration camp or falling into hostile hands. "We had no fear the first time a revolver was pointed at Us," he assured his visitor, "and We shall not have it a second time." In certain situations, he felt, a Pope simply could not remain silent. Alfieri clearly had failed to score.

Roman conversations of one kind or another continued up to the arrest of Dr. Müller in April 1943. But they were at bottom no more than exchanges of views between his associates of the Oster circle, such as Dohnanyi and Bonhoeffer, and his friends in the Eternal City. Of Vatican exchanges in the true sense we cannot speak after January 1940. On the accuracy of this, Father Leiber always said, he would "allow himself to be burned [Dafür lasse ich mich verbrennen]." With the Pope he never again spoke a single word about the matter.[4] The topic obviously had no happy memories for either of them.

Yet, deeply disappointed as he was, the Pope did not hold any resentment at the way he had been led to expect too much and thus to expose the Church and himself to grave dangers. Perhaps the repeated and always accurate string of warnings that reached him did much to reconcile him, as is hinted by a notation in the hand of Tardini, discovered in the Vatican archives in 1966. Completely innocent of any knowledge of the exchanges, he had called the Pope's attention on May 9 to a news item broadcast the previous evening by the American CBS network. This re-

---

[4] Leiber interviews, August 26, 1960, and later.

ported that the Italian Crown Princess, after a visit to the Vatican, had written to a Belgian friend to warn her of a coming invasion. When Tardini wondered whether there could be truth in the story, the Pope confirmed it, saying that he had the information from an anti-Nazi source, and that he was sure of its accuracy since a previous warning with respect to Scandinavia had proved to be exact.[5]

Of even greater interest is an addition to the same notation made by Tardini in 1946. At that time he reminded the Pope of their May 1940 conversation, and Pius replied that he recalled it very well indeed, the more so since the same source had again proved helpful in affording information about the attack on the Soviet Union.[6] The source in question, said the Pontiff, was *Canaris*.

It is clear that those with whom Müller talked in Rome had but a vague idea of the structure of the group he represented. No doubt they heard from time to time of Canaris' dramatic role of guardian angel, but had no notion of the vital part played by Oster. It would have been too much to expect them to understand the complicated relationships at Tirpitz Ufer or to comprehend the unique personality and position of Canaris. Father Leiber affirmed that he had assured the Pope that the warnings led back to Canaris,[7] and their association with that legendary figure, however inaccurate, made them the more impressive.

So Pius maintained his benevolent attitude toward men who, though failing, had not failed him. In their first private audience after the war he received the miraculously surviving Josef Müller with an embrace and the assurance that he had prayed for him

---

[5] The author is indebted to a confidential source for the gist of Tardini's notations. It is noteworthy for Tardini's question to the Pope that at a time when two days before his colleague, Montini, had delivered the warnings to the French and British, he himself knew neither of this nor of the warnings the Pope had given the Low Countries a week earlier. This is additional evidence of the extreme reticence of Pius XII.

[6] Father Leiber, who could not recall the April warning on Scandinavia, remembered with great clarity the one which concerned the attack in the East in 1941. In fact, in the latter case, he had a number of notices as plans developed, probably even as early as late 1940. Interview, April 9, 1966.

[7] Ibid.

every day after hearing of his imprisonment. "We have contended," he said, "with diabolical forces."[8] After the spring of 1940, however, he fought shy of commitments to the German Opposition.

[8] Müller interview, March 31, 1958, and other conversations.

PART FOUR

Documents:

Relevant Papal Pronouncements

Pius XI On the Corporative State
Quadragesimo anno
May 15, 1931

The signing of the Lateran accords on February 11, 1929, between Italy and the Holy See, terminated half a century of severed diplomatic relations and marked the high point of friendly relations between Mussolini and Pius XI. Soon, however, a couple of significant differences developed between the would-be totalitarian Fascist state and the authoritarian Roman Catholic Church. One focused on the Church's disagreement with the Fascist model of the "corporative state." The other involved the Fascist regime's fear of the Catholic organization of the laity, Azione Cattolica (Catholic Action), and of Church-sponsored youth organizations that competed with those of Mussolini.

On May 15, 1931, Pius XI issued the encyclical Quadragesimo anno. *This letter to the bishops marked the fortieth anniversary of* Rerum novarum, *the basic papal pronouncement on the nature of modern industrial society. The advent of the Depression gave the message unusual interest.* Quadragesimo anno *reaffirmed the central principles of that document and sought to bring them up to date. Like its forerunner,* Quadragesimo anno *was sharply critical of traditional capitalism for its exploitation of the working classes, and it approved state intervention to cor-*

SOURCE. *Quadragesimo anno,* May 15, 1931, Encyclical Letter of His Holiness Pius XI on Reconstructing the Social Order and Perfecting It Conformably to the Precepts of the Gospel, in Commemoration of the Fortieth Anniversary of the Encyclical *Rerum novarum,* printed in Oswald von Nell-Breuning, S. J., *Reorganization of Social Economy: The Social Encyclicals Developed and Explained* (Milwaukee: Bruce Publ. Co., 1936–37) , pp. 423–426 *passim.* Reproduced by permission of Bruce Publishing Company.

rect flagrant abuses. It also endorsed the association of laborers in unions for their mutual protection. Ideologically, it took a middle ground between individualism and collectivism. Traditional liberalism "had already shown its utter impotence," the encyclical declared, while socialism was "a remedy much more disastrous than the evil it designed to cure." As a substitute for both of these, Pius XI's message called for harmony between classes. The new papal document was more specific than Rerum novarum *in explaining how this understanding could be achieved. Among the steps it recommended were profit sharing and the establishment of "vocational groups" within each sector of the economy.*

The pope presented these recommendations in such broad terms that Catholics in opposite ideological camps could find in his letter an endorsement of what they were already doing. Thus, economic conservatives interpreted his statement about "vocational groups" to signify self-governing bodies of the corporative type associated with Fascist or quasi-Fascist states. Salazar's Portugal took this line. On the other hand, Christian Democrats of leftist orientation could find in the same encyclical support for their own advocacy of militant social action in favor of the laboring classes. Thus, Quadragesimo anno *faced in two directions, as H. Stuart Hughes has observed.[1] Initially, it seemed more pro-Fascist and antidemocratic than not; but in years to come, when the shams of fascism and corporatism were gradually exposed, the Christian Democratic interpretation came to prevail. Catholics increasingly came to stress the quiet criticism that Pius XI had made of Mussolini's corporatism in practice—of its denial of freedom and its domination by the state. During World War II the principles of* Quadragesimo anno, *explained in this manner, provided inspiration to Christian Democrats who played a militant role in the Resistance movements and, in the early postwar years, stimulated Catholic support of the welfare state.*

The following excerpts from Quadragesimo anno *point up the differences between Pius XI's conception of corporatism and the far more regimented "corporative state" that Mussolini was then erecting.*

[1] H. Stuart Hughes, *Contemporary Europe: A History,* (Englewood Cliffs, N.J.; 3rd rev. ed., 1971), pp. 287–288.

81. Now this is the primary duty of the state and of all good citizens: to abolish conflict between classes with divergent interests, and thus foster and promote harmony between the various ranks of society.

82. The aim of social legislation must therefore be the re-establishment of vocational groups. . . .

85. . . . In these associations the common interests of the whole group must predominate; and among these interests the most important is the directing of the activities of the group to the common good. Regarding cases in which interests of employers and employees call for special care and protection against opposing interests, separate deliberation will take place in their respective assemblies and separate votes will be taken as the matter may require.

86. It is hardly necessary to note that what Leo XIII taught concerning the form of political government can, in due measure, be applied also to vocational groups. Here, too, men may choose whatever form they please, provided that both justice and the common good be taken into account. . . .

91. Within recent times, as all are aware, a special syndical and corporative organization has been inaugurated which, in view of the subject of the present Encyclical, demands of Us some mention and opportune comment.

92. The state here grants legal recognition to the syndicate or union, and thereby confers on it some of the features of a monopoly, for in virtue of this recognition, it alone can represent respectively workingmen and employers, and it alone can conclude labor contracts and labor agreements. Affiliation to the syndicate is optional for everyone; but in this sense only can the syndical organization be said to be free, since the contribution to the union and other special taxes are obligatory for all who belong to a given branch, whether workingmen or employers, and the labor-contracts drawn up by the legal syndicate are likewise obligatory. It is true that it has been authoritatively declared that the legal syndicate does not exclude the existence of unrecognized trade associations.

93. The corporations are composed of representatives of the unions of workingmen and employers of the same trade or profession, and as true and genuine organs and institutions of the state, they direct and co-ordinate the activities of the unions in all matters of common interest.

94. Strikes and lockouts are forbidden. If the contending parties cannot come to an agreement, public authority intervenes.

95. Little reflection is required to perceive the advantage of the institution thus summarily described: peaceful collaboration of the classes, repression of socialist organizations and efforts, the moderating influence of a special ministry.

But in order to overlook nothing in a matter of such importance, and in the light of the general principles stated above, as well as of that which We are now about to formulate, We feel bound to add that to Our knowledge there are some who fear that the state is substituting itself in the place of private initiative, instead of limiting to necessary and sufficient help and assistance. It is feared that the new syndical and corporative institution possesses an excessively bureaucratic and political character, and that, notwithstanding the general advantages referred to above, it risks serving particular political aims rather than contributing to the initiation of a better social order.

96. We believe that to attain this last-named lofty purpose for the true and permanent advantage of the commonwealth, there is need before and above all else of the blessing of God, and, in the second place, of the co-operation of all men of good will. We believe, moreover, as a necessary consequence, that the end intended will be the more certainly attained, the greater the contribution furnished by men of technical, commercial, and social competence, and, more still, by Catholic principles and their application. We look for this contribution, not only to Catholic Action (which has no intention of displaying any strictly syndical or political activities), but to Our sons, whom Catholic Action imbues with these principles and trains for the Apostolate under the guidance and direction of the Church, of the Church, We say, which in the above-mentioned sphere, as in all others where moral questions are discussed and regulated, cannot forget or neglect its mandate as custodian and teacher, given it by God. . . .

Pius XI On Catholic Action
Non abbiamo bisogno
June 29, 1931

The acrimonious dispute between the Italian Fascist regime and Catholic Action simmered along from 1929 until it erupted violently in the spring of 1931. Catholic Action, an organization of the laity, had once again become prominent in Italy when the Catholic Popular party (Partito Popolare Italiano) disintegrated after the advent of the Fascist dictatorship. In 1929 Catholic Action in Italy possessed some 250 diocesan committees, 4000 men's sections, and 5000 youth and university clubs. Determined to control all mass organizations, Mussolini was extremely jealous of Catholic Action, which in many rural areas was stronger than his Fascist party. He therefore sought a pretext to eliminate it, even though he had grudgingly recognized its independence when he signed the Concordat of 1929.

Suddenly in the spring of 1931 Mussolini accused Catholic Action of harboring leaders of the outlawed Popular party and of carrying on social work in competition with Fascist syndical and welfare programs. There was some truth to these charges since Catholic Action, although in no sense an organ of the Populars, did include within its ranks a great many veterans of the disbanded party, and its membership had swelled considerably since 1929—a development that greatly annoyed the Duce. Ramifications of the dispute extended into the university youth organizations. The newly created Fascist University Groups (GUF) attacked the Italian Catholic University Federation (FUCI), and on May 30 the government suppressed the latter. Meanwhile, the Vatican newspaper, L'Osservatore Romano, *skirmished with Mussolini's own newspaper,* Popolo d'Italia, *and chronicled many incidents in which the dictatorship had inter-*

SOURCE. "Encyclical of Pope Pius XI on Catholic Action," in *Sixteen Encyclicals of His Holiness Pope Pius XI, 1926–1937* (Washington, D. C.: National Catholic Welfare Conference, 1938), pp. 1, 7–8, 15, 21–22, 24–25, 27, 30–31. Reprinted by courtesy of the United States Catholic Conference, Washington, D.C.

*fered forcibly with Catholic associations, seizing their publica-
tions, illegally "inspecting" them, and encouraging violence
against individual members.*

On June 29, 1931, Pius XI issued the encyclical Non abbiamo bisogno *("We have no need"), written in vigorous Italian
rather than in Latin in order to emphasize its urgency. He took
elaborate precautions to evade Fascist postal censorship; indeed,
Monsignor Francis Spellman of New York flew several hundred
copies directly from Vatican City to Paris. The text came out in
newspapers abroad before Italians read it on July 5 in
L'Osservatore Romano (which, incidentally, went on sale in the
stands five hours earlier than usual and thus escaped confiscation
until the issue was almost exhausted). The effect was electrify-
ing. The pope had flatly rejected the charge that Catholic Action
leaders were chiefly directors of the defunct Popular party, and
he complained bitterly about the way the Fascists had dissolved
Catholic organizations.*

*On July 9 the Fascist party declared that participation in
Catholic Action was incompatible with party membership;
whereupon thousands resigned from the religious society. On the
other side of the ledger, many Catholic Actionists turned in their
Fascist party cards. The two organizations sparred for another
month or so before reaching a shaky truce on September 2. This
came in the wake of discreet negotiations by Fr. Pietro Tacchi-
Venturi, S.J., and after Mussolini agreed to shove aside two of
his most vocal critics of Catholic Action. There is also evidence
that the* Duce *was disturbed by foreign criticism, and that he had
no desire to unleash an Italian version of Bismarck's* Kulturkampf.

*The chief terms of the compromise were that Catholic Action
was to be diocesan (not national) in character and under direct
control of the bishops (rather than under officers elected by the
members). The bishops would not select its officers from people
who had belonged to "parties hostile to the regime." Professional
sections would not compete with Fascist syndicates, and Catholic
youth organizations would leave athletics to the Fascist entities.
Superficially it seemed as if the dictatorship had triumphed. Nevertheless, the Church could console itself that the society survived and remained independent. Both parties greeted the settlement with unfeigned relief. To demonstrate his satisfaction,*

Mussolini paid an official call on the Holy Father on the third anniversary of the Lateran Pacts; they conversed for more than hour. Next month he ordered the coveted Collar of the Annunciation bestowed upon Eugenio Cardinal Pacelli (the future Pius XII).

Key portions of Pius XI's criticism of Fascist policies follow.

We must needs speak to you, Venerable Brethren, about events which have recently occurred in this, Our Episcopal City of Rome, and throughout Italy, that is to say, in the very territory of which We are Primate—events which have had such a vast and such a strong repercussion everywhere, conspicuously so in all of the dioceses of Italy and throughout the Catholic World.

These occurrences are summarized in a very few and very sad words. There has been an attempt made to strike unto death that which was and that which always will be dearest to Our heart as Father and as Shepherd of Souls; and We can, We even must, subjoin "and the way in which it was done offends Us still more." . . .

Already on several occasions, Venerable Brethren, in the most solemn and explicit manner and assuming entire responsibility for what We were saying, We have protested against the campaign of false and unjust accusations which preceded the disbanding of the associations of the young people and of the university students affiliated with Catholic Action. It was a disbanding which was carried out in a way and with the use of tactics which would give the impression that action was being taken against a vast and dangerous organization of criminals. And the proceedings were directed against young men and young women who are certainly some of the best among the good and concerning whom We are happy and paternally proud to pay them tribute still once more. It is noteworthy that even among the officers of the law charged to carry out these orders of suppressions, there were many who were ill at ease and showed by their expressions and courtesies that they were almost asking pardon for doing that which they had been commanded. We have appreciated the delicate feelings of these officers, and We have reserved for them a special blessing.

However, in sad contrast to the manner of acting of these officials, there were how many acts of mistreatment and of violence, extending even to the striking of blows and the drawing of blood! How many insults in the press, how many injurious words and acts against things and persons, not excluding Ourself, preceded, accompanied and followed the carrying into effect of this lightning-like police order which very frequently, either through ignorance or malicious zeal, was extended to include associations and organizations not contemplated in the orders of the superiors, such as the oratories of the little ones and the sodalities of the Children of Mary. And all of this sad accompaniment of irreverences and of violences took place in the presence of and with the participation of members of a political party some of whom were in uniform, and was carried into effect with such a unison of action throughout all Italy and with such a passive acquiescence on the part of the civil authorities and the police as to make one necessarily think of some uniform directions received from some high authority. It is very easy to admit, and it was also equally easy to have foreseen, that the limits of these directions could and would have almost necessarily been exceeded. . . . We cannot—We, Church, religious, faithful Catholics (and not alone We) —We cannot be grateful to one who, after putting out of existence socialism and anti-religious organizations (Our enemies and not alone Ours), has permitted them to be so generally readmitted, as all see and deplore, and has made them even more strong and dangerous inasmuch as they are now hidden and also protected by their new uniform. . . .

And here We find Ourselves in the presence of a contract between authentic affirmations on the one hand and not less authentic facts on the other hand, which reveal, without the slightest possibility of doubt, the proposal, already in great part actually put into effect, to monopolize completely the young, from the tenderest years up to manhood and womanhood, and all for the exclusive advantage of a party, of a regime based on ideology which clearly resolves itself into a true and real pagan worship of the state, which is no less in contrast with the natural rights of the family than it is in contradiction to the supernatural rights of the Church. To propose and promote such a monopoly, to persecute for this reason Catholic Action, as has been done for some time more or less openly or under cover, to reach this end by striking Catholic Action in the way that has recently occurred, is truly and actually to prevent children from going to Jesus Christ, since it impedes them from going to His Church and even arrives at the point of snatching them with violence from the bosom of both, because where the Church is, there is Jesus Christ. . . .

A conception of the state which makes the young generations belong entirely to it without any exception from the tenderest years up to adult life cannot be reconciled by a Catholic with the Catholic doctrine nor can it be reconciled with the natural right of the family. It is not possible for a Catholic to reconcile with Catholic doctrine the pretense that the Church and the Pope must limit themselves to the external practices of religion, such as Mass and the Sacraments, and then to say that the rest of education belongs to the state. . . .

With everything that We have said up to the present, We have not said that We wished to condemn the party as such. We have intended to point out and to condemn that much in the program and in the action of the party which We have seen and have understood to be contrary to Catholic doctrine and the Catholic practice and therefore irreconcilable with the name and with the profession of Catholics. And in doing this, We have fulfilled a precious duty of Our Episcopal ministry toward Our dear sons who are members of the party, so that they can rest tranquil with the proper consciences of Catholics.

We believe, then, that We have thus at the same time accomplished a good work for the party itself, because what interest and success can the party have in a Catholic country like Italy in maintaining in its program ideas and maxims and practices which cannot be reconciled with a Catholic conscience? . . .

You Bishops of Italy know that no mortal man—not even the head of a state or of a government—but the Holy Ghost—has placed you there in places which Peter assigned to you to rule the Church of God. These and so many other holy and sublime things that concern you, Venerable Brethren, are evidently ignored or forgotten by him who thinks of you and calls you, Bishops of Italy, "Officials of the State," from which the very formula of the oath, which it is necessary for you to make to the sovereign, clearly distinguishes and separates you, for the oath especially states, "as is convenient for a Catholic bishop." . . .

Everything is definitely promised in answer to prayer. . . .

And since from so many prayers We must hope for everything, and since everything is possible to that God Who has promised everything in answer to prayer, We have confident hope that He will illumine minds to Truth and turn wills to Good, so that the Church of God, which wishes nothing from the state that belongs to the competence of the state, will cease to be asked for that which is the Church's competence—the education and the Christian formation of youth—and this not through human favor, but by Divine mandate, and that which therefore she always asks and will always ask with an insistence and an intransigence which cannot cease or waver because it does not come from human desire or design, or from human ideas, changeable in different times and places and circumstances, but from the Divine and inviolable disposition.

Pius XI and Cardinal Pacelli On the Persecution of the Church in Nazi Germany
Mit brennender Sorge ("With deep anxiety")
March 14, 1937

Within a few days of each other in March 1937 Pius XI issued the two most explosive encyclicals of his pontificate: Mit brennender Sorge *on the 14th,* Divini Redemptoris *on the 18th. The first dealt with the situation of the Roman Catholic Church in Nazi Germany; the latter denounced atheistic communism.*

Seven months earlier the German episcopate, assembled in Fulda for its annual conference, had asked the pope for an encyclical regarding the plight of Catholicism in Hitler's Germany.

SOURCE. From *The Persecution of the Catholic Church in the Third Reich: Facts and Documents translated from the German.* London: Burns Oates, 1940. Appendix II, pp. 523–537, *passim.*

Eugenio Cardinal Pacelli, Vatican secretary of state and former nuncio to Germany, conferred in Rome on January 16, 1937, with five of the leading German prelates. Next day they were received by Pius XI himself, although he was still very weak after a prolonged illness. The Holy Father explained that his own sufferings had caused him to understand as never before the sufferings of Christ and the Church, and that he was now convinced an encyclical deploring the situation in Germany must be published as soon as possible. He asked those in attendance to help prepare it. They quickly decided that Michael Cardinal Faulhaber, Archbishop of Munich, should prepare the first draft, and that it should be written in German to underscore its importance. On the 21st Faulhaber brought his version, which began with the words "Mit grosser Sorge" ("With much anxiety"), to Pacelli. The latter, at the pope's request, assumed full responsibility for preparing the final text. Pacelli added not only a full historical introduction regarding the background of the July 20, 1933 Concordat with Hitler's Reich but also certain antiracist passages. The encyclical limited itself to the problems of the rights and privileges of the Catholic Church in Germany, and it sought to avoid a definite breach with the regime; indeed, the pope offered an olive branch to Hitler if he would restore tranquillity to the Church in Germany. Nevertheless, Mit brennender Sorge *stands out as the first great official document to criticize Nazism, and the pope's courage astonished the world. Secretly smuggled into Germany, the letter was read from every Catholic pulpit on Palm Sunday before a single copy fell into the hands of the Nazis.*

Hitler was furious. At his personal order, all copies were to be seized, and anyone found distributing it was to be arrested and dismissed from the Labor Front. Church newspapers in Germany were forbidden to publish it. Soon, however, the Nazi regime decided to stop short of a radical breach with the Catholic Church and instead treated the encyclical with complete silence. Hitler apparently feared that to do otherwise would only make the Catholics more intransigent. Moreover, he probably sensed that millions of German Catholics were giving fairly enthusiastic support to the regime in all matters save those of purely ecclesiastical concern.

The Papal Encyclical
"Mit Brennender Sorge"

ENCYCLICAL LETTER

To the Venerable Archbishops and Bishops and other Ordinaries in Peace and Communism with the Apostolic See: on the Situation of the Catholic Church in Germany

POPE PIUS XI

Venerable Brethren, Greeting and Apostolic Benediction

With deep anxiety and with ever growing dismay We have for a considerable time watched the Church treading the Way of the Cross and the gradually increasing oppression of the men and women who have remained devoted to her in thought and in act in that country and among that people to whom St. Boniface once brought the light of the Gospel of Christ and of the Kingdom of God.

This anxiety of Ours has not been lessened by the reports which the representatives of the reverend Episcopate dutifully and truthfully brought to Us on Our sick-bed. Besides much that is consoling and comforting in the struggle for religion the faithful are now making, they could not, in spite of their love for their people and country and their care to express a balanced judgment, pass silently over too much that is bitter and sad. . . .

When in the summer of 1933, Venerable Brethren, at the request of the German Government We resumed negotiations for a Concordat on the basis of the proposals worked out several years before, and to the satisfaction of you all concluded a solemn agreement. We were moved by the solicitude that is incumbent on Us to safeguard the liberty of the Church in her mission of salvation in Germany and the salvation of the souls entrusted to her—and at the same time by the sincere desire to render an essential service to the peaceful development and welfare of the German people.

In spite of many serious misgivings We then brought Ourselves to decide not to withhold Our consent. We wished to spare

Our loyal sons and daughters in Germany, as far as was humanly possible, the strain and the suffering which otherwise at that time and in those circumstances must certainly have been expected. By Our act We wished to show to all that, seeking only Christ and the things that are Christ's, We refuse to none who does not himself reject it the hand of peace of Mother Church.

If the tree of peace planted by Us with pure intention in German soil has not borne the fruit We desired in the interests of your people, no one in the whole world who has eyes to see or ears to hear can say today that the fault lies with the Church and with her Supreme Head. The experience of the past years fixes the responsibility. It discloses intrigues which from the beginning had no other aim than a war of extermination. In the furrows in which We had laboured to sow the seeds of true peace, others— like the enemy in Holy Scripture (Matt. xiii. 25)—sowed the tares of suspicion, discord, hatred, calumny, of secret and open fundamental hostility to Christ and His Church, fed from a thousand different sources and making use of every available means. On them and on them alone and on their silent and vocal protectors rests the responsibility that now on the horizon of Germany there is to be seen not the rainbow of peace but the threatening storm-clouds of destructive religious wars.

. . . We have done all We could to defend the sanctity of the solemn pledges, the inviolability of obligations freely entered into, against theories and practices which, if officially approved, must destroy all confidence and render intrinsically worthless every future pledge. When the time comes to place before the eyes of the world these endeavours of Ours, all right-minded persons will know where to look for the peace-makers and where to look for the peace-breakers. Anyone who has any sense of truth left in his mind and even a shadow of the feeling of justice left in his heart will have to admit that, in the difficult and eventful years which followed the Concordat, every word and every action of Ours was ruled by loyalty to the terms of the agreement; but also he will have to recognise with surprise and deep disgust that the unwritten law of the other party has been arbitrary misinterpretation of agreements, evasion of agreements, evacuation of the meaning of agreements, and finally more or less open violation of agreements.

Our moderation in spite of all this was not suggested by considerations of human expediency, still less by weakness, but simply by the wish not to root out with the tares any good plant, by the intention not to pronounce a public verdict before minds were ready to recognise its inevitability, by the determination not to deny definitely the loyalty of others to their pledged word, before the iron language of facts had torn away the veil which by deliberate camouflage covered and still covers the attack on the Church. Even today when the open war against the confessional schools, which were guaranteed by the Concordat, and the nullification of the freedom of ballot for those entitled to a Catholic education, show the tragic seriousness of the situation in a field which is a vital interest of the Church and an oppression of the conscience of the faithful such as has never before been witnessed, Our paternal solicitude for the well-being of souls counsels Us not to leave out of consideration any prospects however slight which may still exist of a return to the faithful observance of the pacts and to an agreement permitted by Our conscience. In accordance with the prayers of the most reverend members of the episcopate, we shall not weary in the future of defending violated right before the rulers of your people, unconcerned with temporary success or failure and obedient only to Our conscience and to Our pastoral office, and We shall not cease to oppose an attitude of mind which seeks with open or secret violence to stifle a chartered right.

However, the purpose of the present letter, Venerable Brethren, is different. As you have kindly visited Our sickbed We now turn to you and through you to the faithful Catholics of Germany, who, like all suffering and persecuted children, are very near to the heart of the Common Father. In this hour in which their faith is being tried like true gold in the fire of tribulation, and of secret and open persecution, when they are surrounded by a thousand forms of organised religious bondage, when the lack of truthful news and of normal means of defence weighs heavily upon them, they have a double claim to a word of truth and of spiritual encouragement from him to whose first predecessor Our Saviour addressed these deeply significant words: "But I have prayed for thee, that thy faith fail not; and thou being once converted, confirm thy brethren" (Luke xxii. 32).

True Belief in God

Before all else, Venerable Brethren, see that belief in God, the first and irreplaceable foundation of all religion, remains pure and uncorrupted in German lands. He cannot be considered a believer in God who uses the name of God rhetorically, but he only who unites to that sacred word a true and worthy idea of God. Whoever with pantheistic vagueness identifies God with the universe, and materialises God in the world and deifies the world in God, cannot be reckoned a believer in God. Whoever according to an alleged primitive German pre-Christian conception substitutes a gloomy and impersonal fate for a personal God, denying God's wisdom and providence which "reacheth from end to end mightily and ordereth all things sweetly" (Wisdom viii. 1), cannot claim to be numbered among believers in God.

Whoever transposes Race or People, the State or Constitution, the executive or other fundamental elements of human society (which in the natural order have an essential and honourable place), from the scale of earthly values and makes them the ultimate norm of all things, even of religious values, and deifies them with an idolatrous cult, perverts and falsifies the divinely created and appointed order of things. Such a man is far from true belief in God and from a conception of life in conformity to it. . . .

Only superficial minds can fall into the error of speaking of a national God, of a national religion, and of making a mad attempt to imprison within the frontiers of a single people, within the pedigree of one single race, God, the Creator of the world, the King, and lawgiver of the peoples before whose greatness the nations are as small as drops in a bucket of water (Isaias xl. 15). . . .

We thank you, Venerable Brethren, your priests, and all the faithful who have done and are doing their duty as Christians in defending the rights of the divine Majesty against an aggressive neo-paganism which only too often is supported by influential persons. Our thanks are doubly heartfelt and are combined with a recognition and admiration for those who in doing this duty were thought worthy of enduring temporal sacrifices and temporal sufferings for the cause of God.

True Belief in Christ

. . . The sacred books of the Old Testament are all God's word, an organic part of His revelation. Corresponding to the gradual unfolding of revelation there hangs over them the darkness of the time of preparation for the full noonday of the redemption. As is inevitable with books of history and law, they reflect in many details human imperfection, weakness, and sin. Besides much that is great and noble they relate the materialism and worldliness which appeared again and again in the people of the old covenant, who received the revelation and the promise of God.

. . . Only blindness and self-will can close men's eyes to the treasure of instruction for salvation hidden in the Old Testament. He who wishes to see Bible history and the wisdom of the Old Testament banished from church and school blasphemes the word of God, blasphemes the Almighty's plan of salvation and sets up narrow and limited human thought as the judge of God's plans. He denies faith in Christ who truly appeared in the flesh, and who took His human nature from the people which was afterwards to nail Him to a Cross. He fails completely to understand the world-drama of the Son of God who as high priest set the divine action of His redeeming death in opposition to the evil deeds of those who crucified Him and thus made the Old Testament find in the New its fulfillment, its end, and that by which it is superseded.

The culmination of revelation in the Gospel of Jesus Christ is definitive and obligatory for all time; it admits no additions at the hands of men, and acknowledges no substitute whatever, and no replacement by the arbitrary "revelations" that certain contemporary prophets try to extract from the so-called myth of blood and race. . . . He who sacrilegiously misunderstands the abyss between God and creation, between the God-Man and the children of men, and dares to place beside Christ, or worse still, above Him and against Him, any mortal, even the greatest of all times, must endure to be told that he is a false prophet to whom the words of Scripture find a terrible application: "He that dwelleth in heaven shall laugh at them" (Ps. ii. 4).

True Belief in the Church

. . . The Church founded by the Redeemer is one for all peoples and for all nations; and under its dome, which like the firmament of God stretches over the whole universe, there is a place and home for all peoples and all tongues. . . .

In your territories, Venerable Brethren, voices are raised in an ever louder chorus, urging men to leave the Church, and preachers arise who from their official position try to create the impression that such a departure from the Church and the consequent infidelity to Christ the King is a particularly convincing and meritorious proof of their loyalty to the present régime. By disguised and by open methods of coercion, by intimidation, by holding out prospects of economic, professional, civil or other kinds of advantages, the loyalty of Catholics to their faith, and especially of certain classes of Catholic officials, is subjected to a violence which is as unlawful as it is inhuman. With the feelings of a father We are moved and suffer profoundly with those who have paid such a price for their fidelity to Christ and to the Church; but the point has been reached where it is a question of the last and ultimate end, salvation or perdition, and here the only way of salvation for the believer lies in heroic fortitude. When the tempter or the oppressor approaches with the traitorous suggestion that he should leave the Church, then he can only answer, even at the price of the heaviest earthly sacrifices, in the words of our Saviour: "Begone, Satan: for it is written: The Lord thy God shalt thou adore, and Him only shalt thou serve" (Matt. iv. 10; Luke iv. 8). . . .

True Belief in the Primacy

Belief in the Church will not be kept pure and uncorrupted if it is not supported by belief in the primacy of the Bishop of Rome. . . . When persons who are not even united in faith in Christ entice you and flatter you with the picture of a "German national church," know that that is nothing but a denial of the one Church of Christ, manifest apostasy from the command of

Christ to preach the gospel to the whole world, which can alone
be accomplished by a universal Church. The historical development of other national churches, their spiritual torpor, their sti-
fling by, or subservience to, lay power show the hopeless sterility
which inevitably attacks the branch that separates itself from the
living vine-stem of the Church. Whoever on principle gives to
these false developments a watching and unflinching "No" is ren-
dering a service not only to the purity of his own faith, but also
to the welfare and vitality of his people.

No Transformation of the
Meaning of Sacred Words and Ideas

You must have a specially watchful eye, Venerable Brethren,
when religious ideas are emptied of their real content and are
transformed into a profane meaning. . . .

Moral Doctrine and Moral Order

The morality of the human race is grounded on faith in God
kept true and pure. All attempts to detach the doctrine of moral
law from the granite base of the faith in order to build it up
again on the shifting sands of human regulations sooner or later
bring individuals and nations to moral decadence. . . . The
conscientious observance of the ten commandments of God and
of the precepts of the Church—and these latter are only regulations derived from standards laid down in the Gospels—is for
every individual an incomparable school of systematic discipline,
moral strength, and character-formation. It is a school that asks
much but not too much. . . .

Recognition of the Natural Law

It is a trend of the present day to dissociate more and more,
not only moral teaching, but also the foundations of law and justice from true faith in God and from the revealed commandments of God. Here We have in mind especially what is usually
called natural law, written by the finger of the Creator Himself
on the tables of man's heart (Rom. ii. 14, etc.), which sound hu-

man reason not blinded by sins and passions can read on these tables. By the commandments of this natural law every positive law, whoever may be the lawgiver, can be tested as to its moral content and consequently as to the lawfulness of its authority and as to its obligation in conscience. Those human laws which are irreconcilably opposed to natural law have an innate defect which can be cured neither by compulsion nor by any external display of force. . . .

The believer has an inalienable right to profess his faith and to practise it in the manner suited to him. Laws which suppress or render difficult the profession and practice of this faith are contrary to natural law.

Conscientious parents, aware of their duty in education, have a primary and original God-given right to determine the education of the children given them by God in the spirit of the true faith and in accordance with its fundamental principles and precepts. Laws or other regulations concerning schools, which take no account of the rights of the parents given them by natural law, or which by threats or violence nullify them, contradict the natural law and are essentially immoral.

The Church, the chosen guardian and interpreter of the natural law, cannot do otherwise than declare that the enrolments of pupils which have just taken place in circumstances of notorious coercion are the effects of violence and void of all legality.

To Youth

As the representative of Him who said to a young man in the Gospel: "If thou wilt enter into life keep the commandments" (Matt. xix. 17) We direct especially fatherly words to youth.

By a thousand tongues today there is preached in your ears a gospel which has not been revealed by the heavenly Father: a thousand pens write in the service of a sham Christianity which is not the Christianity of Christ. The printing-press and the radio flood you daily with productions the contents of which are hostile to faith and to Church, and unscrupulously and irreverently attack what, for you, must be sacred and holy.

We know that many, many amongst you, because of your attachment to faith and Church, and because you belong to reli-

gious associations guaranteed by the Concordat, have had to endure, and must still endure, unhappy days of misunderstanding,
of suspicion, of disgrace, of denial of your patriotic loyalty, of
manifold injury to your professional and social life. . . .

No one has any idea of putting stumbling-blocks on the way
leading German youth to the realisation of true national unity, to
the fostering of a noble love of liberty and steadfast loyalty to
their country. What We attack and what We must attack is the
intentional and systematically inspired opposition set up between
these educational aims and the aims of religion. Therefore We
say to this youth: sing your songs of liberty, but do not forget in
them the liberty of the children of God. Do not allow the nobility
of this irreplaceable liberty to pine away in the slave-chains of
sin and sensuality. He who sings the song of loyalty to his earthly
country must not become a deserter and traitor in disloyalty to
his God, his Church, and his heavenly country. You are told
much about heroic greatness, intentionally and falsely contrasted
with the humility and patience of the Gospel; but why are you
not told that there is a heroism in the moral struggle, that to
keep baptismal innocence is a heroic act which ought to be appreciated as it deserves whether in the religious or the natural
sphere? You are told much of human weaknesses in the history
of the Church, but why are you not told of the great deeds which
have accompanied her path across the centuries, the saints she
has produced, the blessing which came to Western civilisation
from the living union between that Church and your people?
You are told a great deal about athletic sports. Practised in moderation and discretion, physical training is beneficial to youth.
But often today so much time is devoted to it that no account is
taken of the complete and harmonious development of body and
spirit, nor of the fitting care of family life, nor of the command-
ment of Sunday observance. With a disregard bordering on indifference the sacred character and peace of the Lord's Day, which
are in the best German tradition, are taken away. We confidently
expect from believing Catholic youth that in the difficult atmos-
phere of compulsory State organisations they will unflinchingly
insist on their right to keep holy the Christian Sunday, that the
care of physical fitness will not make them forget their immortal
souls, that they will not allow themselves to be overcome by evil,

but will strive to overcome evil by good (Rom. xii. 21), that their highest aim will be to obtain the crown of victory in the race for eternal life (1 Cor. ix. 24).

To Priests and Religious

We address a word of special recognition, encouragement, and exhortation to the priests of Germany, on whom, under their bishops, rests the task of showing the flock of Christ in difficult times and in trying circumstances the right paths by daily sacrifice and apostolic patience. . . .

To the Faithful among the Laity

Before Our eyes stand the countless host of Our beloved sons and daughters for whom the suffering of the Church in Germany and their own suffering has in no way affected their devotion to the cause of God, their tender love towards the Father of Christendom, their obedience to their bishops and priests, their joyful readiness to remain in future, come what may, faithful to what they have believed and what they have received as a precious heritage from their forefathers. From a heart deeply moved We send them Our paternal greeting. . . .

Venerable Brethren, We are certain that the words which We in this decisive hour address through you to the Catholics of Germany will awaken in the hearts and in the actions of Our loyal children an echo answering the loving solicitude of their Common Father. If there is anything that We beseech of the Lord with special fervour it is that Our words mảy also reach the ears and the hearts and move to reflection those who have already begun to let themselves be beguiled by the flatteries and threats of the enemies of Christ and of His holy Gospel.

We have weighed every word of this Encyclical in the balance of truth and also of love. Neither did We wish by inopportune silence to be guilty of not having made the situation clear, nor by excessive severity to harden the hearts of those who since they are placed under Our pastoral responsibility are no less the objects of Our pastoral charity because they are now wandering in the paths of error and estrangement. . . .

With this prayer of supplication in Our heart and on Our lips, as a pledge of divine assistance and as a support in your difficult and responsible decisions, as an aid in the struggle, a comfort in sorrow to your bishops, pastors of your faithful people, to the priests, to the religious, to the lay apostles of Catholic Action and to all your diocesans and not least to those who are sick and those in prison, We impart with fatherly love the Apostolic Blessing.

Given at the Vatican on Passion Sunday, March 14th, 1937.

PIUS PP. XI.

Pius XI On Atheistic Communism
Divini redemptoris
March 18, 1937

As the Communist dictatorship in Soviet Russia entrenched it-self more firmly in the 1930s and the Third International spread its propaganda with increasing effectiveness in Spain, Mexico, and elsewhere, Pius XI became ever more concerned about the threat of communism. Thus it was no coincidence that he decid-ed to carefully balance his criticism of Nazi Germany in Mit brennender Sorge *(March 14, 1937) with another encyclical,* Divini redemptoris, *issued four days later, that attacked "atheis-tic communism." This was quickly followed by a third encyclical,* Firmissimam constantiam, *that dealt specifically with religious persecution in Mexico.*

In Divini redemptoris, *Pius XI complained that "fallacious hopes" of Communist inspiration had seduced many people "of no ordinary worth," and that "inexplicable silence" on the part of much of the press had left the world in ignorance of the "evil" perpetrated by communism in Russia, Spain, and Mexico. To the errors of communism the pontiff opposed the doctrines of the Catholic Church. He recalled the economic principles of* Re-rum novarum *and* Quadragesimo anno *and clarified these with greater precision. He went on to declare that it was "of utmost importance to foster in all classes of society an intensive program*

SOURCE. Released at Vatican City; printed by the Associated Press in *The New York Times,* March 19, 1937, p. 10.

*of social education, adapted to the varying degrees of intellectual
culture; and to spare no pains to procure the widest possible diffusion of the social teachings of the Church among all classes, including the workers." These papal admonitions were to have a
strong impact on Catholic education and the development of
Catholic labor unions.*

The Vatican's official abstract in English of Divini redemptoris
follows.

The Official Abstract
of the Pope's Encyclical
By The Associated Press

*VATICAN CITY, March 18.—Following is the Official Vati-
can abstract of Pope Pius's encyclical on atheistic communism,
including the salient points textually:*

The encyclical, divided into chapters and numbered paragraphs, begins by pointing out the serious danger to which all nations are exposed by the inroads of communism.

After recalling how his predecessors and he, himself, had
more than once called the attention of the world to this danger,
the Holy Father asserts the necessity of a new, solemn document.

"Therefore we believe it to be our duty to raise our voice once
more in a still more solemn missive in accordance with the tradition of this Apostolic See, the teacher of truth, and in accordance
with the desire of the whole Catholic world which makes the appearance of such a document natural.

"We trust that the echo of our voice will reach every mind free
from prejudice and every heart sincerely desirous of the good of
mankind.

"We wish this still the more because our words are now re-
ceiving sorry confirmation from the spectacle of the bitter fruits
of subversive ideas which we foresaw and foretold, and which
are multiplying fearfully in countries already stricken, or threatening every other country in the world.

"The doctrine of communism was founded on the principles of dialectical and historical materialism previously advocated by Marx, of which the theoreticians of bolshevism claim to possess the only genuine interpretation.

Essence of the Doctrine

"According to this doctrine, there is in the world only one reality, matter, the blind forces of which evolve into plant, animal and man.

"Even human society is nothing but phenomena and a form of matter evolving in the same way. By the law of inexorable necessity and through the perpetual conflict of forces, matter moves toward the final synthesis of a classless society.

"In such a doctrine, as is evident, there is no room for the idea of God; there is no difference between matter and spirit, between soul and body; there is neither the survival of the soul after death nor any hope of a future life.

"Thus, man's liberty is destroyed. Every right of the human person is denied. Man becomes, as it were, a mere cog in the collectivist machinery which alone has unlimited control over the lives of men. All hierarchy, all authority is nullified.

"The dignity and indissolubility of marriage are set aside. The family is profaned. The woman is torn from her home and from the care of her children. Religion is dubbed the opiate of the people and assailed with any weapon at hand. The very idea of God is rejected and condemned.

"Communism, therefore, is a system full of errors and sophisms. It is in opposition to both reason and divine revelation.

"It is subversive to the social order because it means the destruction of its foundations; because it ignores the true origin and purpose of the State; and because it denies the right, dignity and liberty of human personality."

That a system so obviously erroneous should be so widely accepted is due to the false idea of justice and equality which communism has held up to the masses, promising elimination of many undeniable abuses and improvement of the condition of the poor workingman.

Deceived by the theses and promises, they have blindly followed the prophets of the new doctrine, unable to perceive the very serious errors of communism.

"By pretending to desire only betterment of the condition of the working classes, by urging removal of the very real abuses chargeable to a liberalistic economic order and by demanding a more equitable distribution of this world's goods (an objective entirely and undoubtedly legitimate), the Communists take advantage of the present world-wide crisis to draw into the sphere of their influence even those sections of the populace which on principle reject all forms of materialism and terrorism."

Other Causes of Trend

In addition to the sad plight in which liberal economics have left the workingman, two other factors undoubtedly hastened this diffusion: clever, widespread propaganda organized with truly diabolical perfection and the inexplicable silence of a large section of the press in the face of the spread of communism.

Meanwhile the sad effects of the evil already are evident in several nations, such as Mexico and Spain, and especially Russia, which was chosen, so to speak, as the ground for this new doctrine.

To the real Russian people, saddened and oppressed, the Holy Father offers an expression of his paternal sympathy.

"In making these observations it is no part of our intention to condemn en masse the peoples of the Soviet Union. For them we cherish the warmest paternal affection. We are well aware that not a few of them groan beneath the yoke imposed on them by men who in a very large part are strangers to the real interests of the country.

"We recognize many others have been deceived by these fallacious hopes. We blame only the system, with its authors and abettors, who considered Russia the best-prepared field for experimenting with a plan elaborated decades ago, and who from there continue to spread it from one end of the world to the other."

To the errors of communism the Pontiff opposes the doctrines of the Catholic Church, which, acknowledging its God as a creator, judge and loving father, proclaims the equality of the brotherhood of man and defends the liberty of man and the rights of the human person.

Destined by God for a supernatural end of eternal happiness, man should find in domestic and civil society, both ordained by God, due respect for his personal rights and help to facilitate the attainment of his sublime destiny.

On the basis of these principles the church recognizes and defends a hierarchy and the legitimate authority of society, which can and should use its influence even in the field of social economics.

Proposing opportune social norms, it (society) should be a directive and coordinating force and even use legal means of constraint and repression when the activity of individuals or groups may tend to the detriment of the common good.

"This doctrine is equally removed from all extremes of error and all exaggerations of parties or systems which stem from error. It maintains the constant equilibrium of truth and justice, which it vindicates in theory and promotes and applies in practice, bringing into harmony the rights and duties of all parties.

How Balance Is Struck

"Thus authority is reconciled with the liberty and dignity of the individual and with that of the State, the human personality of the subject with the divine delegation of the superior; and in this way a balance is struck between the due dependence and well-ordered love of man for himself, his family and his country, his love of other families and other people, founded on the love of God, father of all, their first principle and last end.

"The church does not separate the proper regard for temporal welfare from solicitude for the eternal. If she subordinates the former to the latter—according to the words of her divine founder, 'Seek ye first the kingdom of God and His justice, and all these things shall be added unto you'—she is nevertheless so far from being unconcerned with human affairs and so far from hindering civil progress and material advancement that she actually fosters and promotes them in the most sensible and efficacious manner.

"Thus, even in the field of social economics, and although the church has never proposed a definite technical system, since this is not her field, she nevertheless has clearly outlined the guiding principles which, while susceptible to varied concrete application according to diversified conditions of times, places and peoples, indicate a safe way of securing happy progress for society.

"The church has always acted in conformity with this doctrine, in spite of the greatest of difficulties and enduring bitter persecution in her defense of the truth."

After this point the Holy Father proposes remedies to be applied against very grave modern ills, remedies which he epitomizes by inviting all his children to a renewal of Christian life.

Lukewarm Are Chided

"Even in Catholic countries there are still too many who are Catholic hardly more than in name. There are too many who fulfill more or less faithfully the more essential obligations of the religion they boast of professing, but have no desire for knowing it better or deepening their inward convictions and still less of bringing into conformity with the external gloss the inner splendor of an unsullied conscience that recognizes and performs all its duties under the eye of God."

In particular, the Holy Father recommends to the faithful detachment from worldly goods, Christian charity and especially justice; detachment from worldly possessions, for these do not constitute man's true goods; Christian charity, which should move all to commiserate and help those who suffer; justice above all, which should induce employers and the wealthy to recognize the inalienable right of the working-man to a wage sufficient for himself and his family and safeguard, even in labor, his lofty dignity as a man and child of God.

"The wage-earner is not to receive as alms what is his due in justice; let no one attempt with trifling charitable donations to exempt himself from the great duties imposed by justice.

"Both justice and charity often dictate obligations touching upon the same subject matter but under different aspects; and the very dignity of the workingman makes him justly and acutely sensitive to the duties of others in this regard."

The Pope then recommends a better understanding and fuller study of the doctrine of the church, which alone, in the name of Jesus Christ, can point out the path to true civil progress.

Action must be joined to study if the Communist enterprise is to be effectively resisted.

"Communism is intrinsically wrong and no one who would save Christian civilization may collaborate with it in any undertaking whatsoever.

"Those who permit themselves to be deceived into lending their aid toward the triumph of communism in their own country will first fall as victims to their error.

"And because of the greater antiquity and grandeur of Christian civilization in the regions where communism successfully penetrates, so much more devastating will be the hatred displayed by the godless."

In the front line of this battle against communism, says the Holy Father, should stand the priests, whose duty it is to show the way to all others by word and example. Catholic Action also should distinguish itself particularly in this field, aided by those other religious groups which the Holy Father has himself called auxiliary organizations.

Other Organizations Rallied

Nor does the Pontiff forget other organizations which should be inspired by principles of a sound, well-planned social order. After a special appeal to Catholics, workers and non-workers, to put aside their vain trifling differences and unite in this great struggle, the Holy Father pleads with all those who believe in God to resist the furious attack of the godless.

Even the State should play a part in the attainment and hope for victory by aiding the activity of the church, by adopting timely measures and by giving an example of wise, prudent administration.

"This means all diligence should be exercised by States to prevent within their territory the ravages of the anti-God campaign, which shakes society to its very foundations.

"For there can be no authority on earth unless the authority of divine majesty be recognized; no oath will bind which is sworn in the name of a living 'god.' "

The Holy Father then makes this heartfelt appeal to his erring children:

"We cannot conclude this encyclical letter without addressing some words to those of our children who are more or less tainted with the Communist plague.

"We earnestly exhort them to hear the voice of their loving father. We pray the Lord to enlighten them that they may abandon the slippery path which will precipitate one and all to ruin and catastrophe and that they recognize Jesus Christ our Lord as their only Saviour. 'For there is no other name under heaven given to man whereby we must be saved.' "

The encylical closes with an exhortation to all to turn their thoughts to St. Joseph, powerful protector of the church, living model of that Christian justice which should reign in the social life.

Pius XII On the Limitations of the Authority of the State
Summi pontificatus
October 20, 1939

On October 20, 1939, the recently crowned Pius XII published his first encyclical, Summi pontificatus, *a carefully thought-out document that is fundamental for understanding how he conceived his mission. The letter sought to point out to the world the basis on which a spiritual rebirth must rest. To many it was a message of light and truth in a world that had been dislocated by the outbreak of war less than two months before. Emphasizing the need for peace, Pius XII declared that he had left nothing untried, within the forms consonant to his apos-*

SOURCE. Excerpts from text printed in *The Papal Encyclicals in Their Historical Context,* edited by Anne Fremantle. New York: Mentor Books, 1956, pp. 265–269.

tolic office, to prevent the recourse to arms. He promised to continue to do everything possible to promote conciliation.

Although the message was couched in language that transcended, for the most part, problems of specific nations, one long section, excerpted below, was especially relevant to the totalitarian regimes of that era. In these paragraphs Pius XII set forth his views regarding the limits of the authority of the state in the modern world. These were further developed in his Christmas Eve message of 1945, referred to earlier by Mr. McKnight on pages 37–38.

* * * *

. . . But there is yet another error no less pernicious to the well-being of the nations and to the prosperity of that great human society which gathers together and embraces within its confines all races. It is the error contained in those ideas which do not hesitate to divorce civil authority from every kind of dependence upon the Supreme Being—First Source and absolute Master of man and of society—and from every restraint of a Higher Law derived from God as from its First Source. Thus they accord the civil authority an unrestricted field of action that is at the mercy of the changeful tide of human will, or of the dictates of casual historical claims, and of the interests of a few.

Once the authority of God and the sway of His law are denied in this way, the civil authority as an inevitable result tends to attribute to itself that absolute autonomy which belongs exclusively to the Supreme Maker. It puts itself in the place of the Almighty and elevates the State or group into the last end of life, the supreme criterion of the moral and juridical order, and therefore forbids every appeal to the principles of natural reason and of the Christian conscience. . . .

* * * *

. . . It is the noble prerogative and function of the State to control, aid and direct the private and individual activities of national life that they converge harmoniously towards the common good. That good can neither be defined according to arbitrary ideas nor can it accept for its standard primarily the material prosperity of society, but rather it should be defined according to the harmonious development and the natural perfection of man. It is for this perfection that society is designed by the Creator as a means.

To consider the State as something ultimate to which everything else should be subordinated and directed, cannot fail to harm the true and lasting prosperity of nations. This can happen either when unrestricted dominion comes to be conferred on the State as having a mandate from the nation, people, or even a social order, or when the State arrogates such dominion to itself as absolute master, despotically, without any mandate whatsoever. If, in fact, the State lays claim to and directs private enterprises, these, ruled as they are by delicate and complicated internal principles which guarantee and assure the realization of their special aims, may be damaged to the detriment of the public good, by being wrenched from their natural surroundings, that is, from responsible private action. . . .

* * * *

True courage and a heroism worthy in its degree of admiration and respect, are often necessary to support the hardships of life, the daily weight of misery, growing want and restrictions on a scale never before experienced, whose reason and necessity are not always apparent. Whoever has the care of souls and can search hearts knows the hidden tears of mothers, the resigned sorrow of so many fathers, the countless bitternesses of which no statistics tell or can tell. He sees with sad eyes the mass of suffering ever on the increase; he knows how the powers of disorder and destruction stand on the alert ready to make use of all these things for their dark designs. No one of good-will and vision will think of refusing the State, in the exceptional conditions of the world today, correspondingly wider and exceptional rights to meet the popular needs. But even in such emergencies, the moral law, established by God, demands that the lawfulness of each such measure and its real necessity be scrutinized with the greatest rigor according to the standards of the common good.

In any case, the more burdensome the material sacrifices demanded of the individual and the family by the State, the more must the rights of conscience be to it sacred and inviolable. Goods, blood it can demand; but the soul redeemed by God, never. The charge laid by God on parents to provide for the material and spiritual good of their offspring and to procure for them a suitable training saturated with the true spirit of religion, cannot be wrested from them without grave violations of their rights. . . .

* * * *

The idea which credits the State with unlimited authority is not simply an error harmful to the internal life of nations, to their prosperity, and to the larger and well-ordered increase in their well-being, but likewise it injures the relations between peoples, for it breaks the unity of supranational society, robs the law of nations of its foundation and vigor, leads to violation of others' rights and impedes agreement and peaceful intercourse.

A disposition, in fact, of the divinely sanctioned natural order divides the human race into social groups, nations or States, which are mutually independent in organization and in the direction of their internal life. But for all that, the human race is bound together by reciprocal ties moral and juridical, into a great commonwealth directed to the good of all nations and ruled by special laws which protect its unity and promote its prosperity.

Now no one can fail to see how the claim to absolute autonomy for the State stands in open opposition to this natural way that is inherent in man—nay, denies it utterly—and therefore leaves the stability of international relations at the mercy of the will of rulers, while it destroys the possibility of true union and fruitful collaboration directed to the general good.

So, Venerable Brethren, it is indispensable for the existence of harmonious and lasting contacts and of fruitful relations, that the peoples recognize and observe these principles of international natural law which regulate their normal development and activity. Such principles demand respect for corresponding rights to independence, to life and to the possibility of continuous development in the paths of civilization; they demand, further, fidelity to compacts agreed upon and sanctioned in conformity with the principles of the law of nations.

The indispensable presupposition, without doubt, of all peaceful intercourse between nations, and the very soul of the juridical relations in force among them, is mutual trust: the expectation and conviction that each party will respect its plighted word; the certainty that both sides are convinced that "Better is wisdom, than weapons of war" *(Ecclesiastes ix: 18)*, and are ready to enter into discussion and to avoid recourse to force or to threats of force in case of delays, hindrances, changes or disputes, because all these things can be the result not of bad-will but of changed circumstances and of genuine interests in conflict.

But on the other hand to tear the law of nations from its anchor in Divine law, to base it on the autonomous will of States, is to dethrone that very law and deprive it of its noblest and strongest qualities. Thus it would stand abandoned to the fatal drive of private interest and collective selfishness exclusively intent on the assertion of its own rights and ignoring those of others.

Now, it is true that with the passage of time and the substantial change of circumstances, which were not and perhaps could not have been foreseen in the making of a treaty, such a treaty or some of its clauses can in fact become, or at least seem to become, unjust, impracticable or too burdensome for one of the parties. It is obvious that should such be the case, recourse should be had in good time to a frank discussion with a view to modifying the treaty or making another in its stead. But to consider treaties on principle as ephemeral and tacitly to assume the authority of rescinding them unilaterally when they are no longer to one's advantage, would be to abolish all mutual trust among States. In this way, natural order would be destroyed and there would be seen dug between different peoples and nations trenches of division impossible to refill.

Today, Venerable Brethren, all men are looking with terror into the abyss to which they have been brought by the errors and principles which We have mentioned, and by their practical consequences. Gone are the proud illusions of limitless progress. . . .

Pius XII On National Socialism
Allocution to the Sacred College of Cardinals
June 2, 1945

Many critics have complained that Pope Pius XII never saw fit during the war to speak out publicly against the moral evil of National Socialism. Whether he was justified in exercising such reserve is something for the individual reader to consider. In fairness to Pius XII, however, it should be noted that three weeks after the end of the conflict in Europe, he did speak out unmistakably against National Socialist doctrines. In an allocution to the Sacred College of Cardinals in the Vatican on June 2, 1945, he referred specifically to the German people:

"We nourish faith that they can restore themselves to new dignity and to new life, now that they have rejected the satanic specter of National Socialism, and after the guilty parties (as We have already had occasion to explain elsewhere) have expiated the crimes they have committed. . . .

"In order to resist such attacks, millions of valorous Catholics, men and women alike, rallied around their Bishops, whose courageous and stern voice never ceased to speak out right through these final years of the war; and rallied around their priests, in order to help them continuously adapt their apostolate to changing needs and circumstances. Against the forces of impiety and pride they resisted to the very end with patience and firmness in their faith, their prayers, their conduct, and their frankly Catholic education. . . .

"We Ourselves during the war, particularly in Our Messages, never ceased to set forth the uncompromising standards and demands of both humanity and the Christian faith against the ruinous and inexorable application of National Socialist doctrines, which even went so far as to make use of the most refined scientific methods to torture and kill persons who often were quite innocent. . . ."

SOURCE. Cited in Ernesto Rossi, *Il Manganello e l'aspersorio* [The Cudgel and the Aspergillum] (Florence, 1948), pp. 460–461. My translation.

SUGGESTIONS FOR FURTHER READING

Since much of this historical controversy was greatly stimulated by Rolf Hochhuth's explosive drama, *Der Stellvertreter* (Reinbek bei Hamburg, 1963), it is appropriate to mention, first of all, the English edition of this play, *The Deputy* (New York, 1964), translated by Richard and Clara Winston and including the playwright's explanatory sidelights on history. This should be supplemented by Eric Bentley (ed.), *The Storm over "The Deputy"* (New York, 1964), an anthology of perceptive essays and articles about Hochhuth's drama.

The appearance of Hochhuth's play almost certainly hastened the publication of a series of volumes of fascinating and indispensable documents from the archives of the Holy See that clarify its relationship to World War II: Secrétairerie d'État de Sa Sainteté, *Actes et Documents du Saint Siège relatifs à la Seconde Guerre Mondiale* (Vatican City, 1965–). Thus far, seven volumes have appeared, covering the papacy's role through December 1943. In addition to official correspondence between the Holy See and various governments, the series includes letters from Pope Pius XII to the German bishops and reports on the religious situation in Poland and the Baltic countries, and documents illustrating the papacy's efforts to help war victims from 1939 to December 1940. An English translation of this series, *Records and Documents of the Holy See relating to the Second World War,* is being prepared by Gerard Noel for Herder Publications, London, and Corpus Books, Washington-Cleveland. The official documentary collections on the foreign relations of Italy, Germany, Britain, and the United States are also of value, as is Myron C. Taylor (ed.), *Wartime Correspondence between President Roosevelt and Pope Pius XII* (New York, 1947). One should also note the memoirs of the French ambassador to the Holy See, François Charles-Roux, *Huit ans au Vatican, 1932–1940* (Paris, 1947), and the diaries of Count Galeazzo Ciano, who was Italian Foreign Minister from 1936 to 1943. A number of documents from the files of the German Embassy to the Holy See were published in 1964 in French, with commentary, by Saul A. Friedlaender, whose parents had been killed at Auschwitz. The English version of Friedlaender's book, translated by Charles Fullman, bears the title *Pius XII and the Third Reich: A Documentation* (New York, 1966). The protests of the Holy See to the Third Reich over the latter's violation of the 1933 Concordat are to be found in Dieter Albrecht (ed.), *Der Notenwechsel zwischen dem Heiligen Stuhl und der deutschen Reichsregierung: Tome I, Von der Ratifizierung des Reichskonkordate bis zur Enzyklika "Mit brennender Sorge"* (Mainz, 1965). Of similar interest is the collection, translated from the German, *The Persecution of the Catholic Church in the Third Reich: Facts and Documents* (London, 1940).

Among the studies that focus primarily on Germany, one should consult John S. Conway, *The Nazi Persecution of the Churches, 1933–45* (New York and London, 1968), written by a Catholic historian; Guenter Lewy, *The Catholic Church and Nazi Germany* (New York and Toronto, 1964), which deals with the Old Reich, exclusive of Austria and other territories later acquired by Nazi Germany; Mary Alice Gallin, *German Resistance to Hitler: Ethical and Religious Factors* (Washington, 1961); Nathaniel Micklem, *National Socialism and the Roman Catholic Church* (London, 1939); J. Rovan, *Le Catholicisme politique en Allemagne* (Paris, 1956); Michele Maccarone, *Il nazionalsocialismo e la Santa Sede* (Rome, 1947); and Fr. Angelo Martini, S. J., "Il Cardinale Faulhaber e l'enciclica 'Mit brennender Sorge'," *Archivum Historiae Pontificiae* (Rome), II (1964), pp. 303–320. Portions of the following are also of use: Karl Dietrich Bracher, *The German Dictatorship: The Origins, Structure, and Effects of National Socialism,* translated by Jean Steinberg (New York, 1970); Hans Rothfels, *The German Opposition to Hitler: An Assessment,* translated by Lawrence Wilson (London, 1961); Terence Prittie, *Germans against Hitler* (Boston, 1964), and Kurt Meier, *Die Deutschen Christen: Das Bild einer Bewegung im Kirchenkampf des Dritten Reiches* (Halle, 1964); and Franz von Papen, *Memoirs* (London, 1953).

On World War II developments, see especially Harold C. Deutsch's carefully researched book, *The Conspiracy against Hitler in the Twilight War* (Minneapolis, 1968); Owen Chadwick's critical review, "The Papacy and World War II," *Journal of Ecclesiastical History*, XVIII, No. 1 (April, 1967), pp. 71–79; Camille M. Cianfarra's journalistic observations in Rome, *The Vatican and the War* (New York, 1944); Paul Duclos, *Le Vatican et la Seconde Guerre Mondiale* (Paris, 1955); the Communist interpretation of Mikhail Markovich Sheinmann, *Der Vatikan im Zweiten Weltkrieg* (Berlin, 1954); Charles F. Delzell's article, "Italy, Pius XII, and the War," *Journal of Contemporary History*, II, No. 4 (1967), pp. 137–161; and Fr. Alberto Giovannetti's well-informed *Il Vaticano e la guerra (1939–1940): Note storiche* (Vatican City, 1960).

The role of the Jews is taken up sympathetically by Pinchas E. Lapide, *Three Popes and the Jews* (New York, 1967), which can be supplemented by Eliahu Ben Elissar, *La Diplomatie du III* *Reich et les Juifs (1933–1939)* (Paris, 1969). Carlo Falconi has written *The Silence of Pius XII,* translated by Bernard Wall (Boston, 1970), which focuses especially on the persecution of Jews in Yugoslavia and central Europe. Jenö Levai, *Geheime Reichssache: Papst Pius XII hat nicht geschwiegen* (Cologne, 1965) deals with the Holy See and Hungary. Of general scope are Raul Hilberg (comp.), *Documents of Destruction: Germany and Jewry, 1933–1945* (Chicago, 1971), and his earlier study, *The Destruction of the European Jews* (Chicago, 1961); Gerald Reitlinger, *The Final Solution* (New York, 1953); Leon Poliakov, *Harvest of Hate* (London, 1965); and Marie Joseph Congar, *The Catholic Church and the Race Question* (Paris, 1953).

For relations with the Soviet Union one can consult Camille M. Cianfarra, *The Vatican and the Kremlin* (New York, 1950), written during the Cold War by a *New York Times* correspondent in Rome; and Maxime Mourin, *Le Vatican et l'U.R.S.S.* (Paris, 1966), which is critical of the Holy See.

Numerous studies deal with the relationship of the Roman Catholic Church to Fascist Italy. The best place to begin is the careful study by an Irish Catholic, Daniel A. Binchy, *Church and State in Fascist Italy* (Oxford, 1941; reprinted 1970). Arturo Carlo Jemolo, an Italian liberal Catholic, has condensed a longer study into *Chiesa e Stato in Italia: Dalla unificazione a Giovanni XXIII* (Turin, 1965). An earlier edition, with shorter time span, was the basis for *Church and State in Italy,*

1850–1950, translated by David Moore (Oxford, 1960). Jemolo's
student, Francesco Margiotta Broglio, has written *Italia e Santa
Sede dalla Grande Guerra alla Conciliazione* (Bari, 1966). Excellent, too, is Richard A. Webster, *The Cross and the Fasces:
Christian Democracy and Fascism in Italy* (Stanford, 1960).
Luigi Salvatorelli and Giovanni Mira, *Storia d'Italia nel periodo
fascista* (Turin, 1962), is the standard history of the Fascist era
from a liberal standpoint. Charles F. Delzell, *Mussolini's Enemies* (Princeton, 1961), deals with the anti-Fascist opposition
and the Resistance and gives considerable attention to the Catholics. His *Mediterranean Fascism, 1919–1945* (New York, 1970
provides documentation and commentary on Italy, Spain,
and Portugal. Pietro Scoppola has edited *Chiesa e il Fascismo:
Documenti e interpretazioni* (Bari, 1971), a careful study. The
last chapter of Scoppola's *Coscienza religiosa e democrazia
nell'Italia contemporanea* (Bologna, 1966) also deals with the
Fascist era. Strongly anticlerical was the late Ernesto Rossi's *Il
manganello e l'aspersorio* [The Cudgel and the Aspergillum]
(Florence, 1948). The anthology of Frances Keene (ed.), *Neither Liberty Nor Bread* (New York, 1940), contains critical articles by Carlo Sforza, "Pius XI, the Roman Church and Fascism," and Gaetano Salvemini, "Vatican and Ethiopian War."
The brother of Pius XII played a major role in negotiating the
Lateran accords of 1929, as he has revealed in his diary: Francesco Pacelli, *Diario della Conciliazione* (Vatican City, 1959).
Broader treatments of Church-State problems in Italy are to be
found in Vittorio Gorresio (ed.), *Stato e Chiesa* (Bari, 1957);
S. William Halperin, *The Separation of Church and State in Italian Thought from Cavour to Mussolini* (Chicago, 1937); and P.
Vincent Bucci, *Chiesa e Stato: Church-State Relations in Italy
within the Contemporary Constitutional Framework* (The Hague,
1969). Written before the overthrow of fascism, *What To Do
with Italy* (New York, 1943), by George LaPiana and Gaetano
Salvemini, is quite critical of the Church. More charitable is Luigi Sturzo, *Italy and the Coming World* (New York, 1945).

The seventh volume of *Actes et Documents du Saint Siège relatifs
à la Seconde Guerre Mondiale,* published in 1973, focuses on relations with Italy at the time of the overthrow of the Fascist dictatorship in 1943 and on the pope's efforts to spare Rome from

bombing. In addition, see the staunchly pro-Vatican books of
Giulio Castelli, *Il Vaticano nei tentacoli del fascismo* (Rome,
1946) ; *La Chiesa e il fascismo* (Rome, 1951) ; and *Storia segre-
ta di Roma città aperta* (Rome, 1959). In the same vein is Alberto Giovannetti, *Roma città aperta* (Milan, 1962). Other
books that shed light from a different perspective on the period
when Rome was an "open city" during the German occupation
(September 1943–June 1944) and the Jews were being rounded
up by the Nazis are Eugen Dollmann, *Roma nazista* (Milan,
1949), written by a high German official in Rome; R. Perrone
Capano, *La Resistenza in Roma* (Naples, 1963) ; and Robert
Katz, *Death in Rome* (New York, 1967). The last-named book,
which deals with the March 1944 massacre of 335 Italians (of
whom 176 were Jews) in Rome's Ardeatine Caves and is very
hostile toward Pius XII, has recently been made into a movie in
Italy, with Richard Burton. One should also consult the article of
Mario Benedetti, "Il comportamento della Santa Sede durante i
venti mesi dell'occupazione tedesca d'Italia," in Ruggero Zan-
grandi, *1943: 25 luglio-8 settembre* (Milan, 1964), pp. 1072–1077.

The standard work on the history of the Italian Jews under
Mussolini's dictatorship is Renzo De Felice, *Storia degli ebrei
italiani sotto il fascismo* (Turin, 1961). De Felice is also the author of a massive biography of the life and times of Mussolini,
the third volume of which has a long chapter on the Conciliation
of 1929: *Mussolini il fascista: L'organizzazione dello Stato fascista, 1925–1929* (Turin, 1968). Shorter discussions may be
found in such English-language biographies as Ivone Kirkpatrick, *Mussolini: A Study in Power* (New York, 1964), and
Laura Fermi, *Mussolini* (Chicago, 1961). Herman Finer, *Mussolini's Italy* (London, 1935; reprint, New York, 1965), has a
section dealing with Church and State.

One of the most informative and critical studies of the various
popes of this era is Carlo Falconi, *The Popes in the Twentieth
Century: From Pius X to John XXIII,* translated from the
Italian by Muriel Grindrod (London, 1967). Philip Hughes,
Pope Pius XI (London, 1937), although published before the
pontiff's death, is a useful study, as is Mgr. R. Fontenelle, *His
Holiness Pope Pius XI,* translated by M. E. Fowler (London,
1939). These can be supplemented by Fr. Angelo Martini, S. J.,

"Gli ultimi giorni di Pio XI," *Civiltà Cattolica* (1959), No. 4, 236–250, which illuminates the last phase of Pius XI's reign. Luigi Salvatorelli, *Pio XI e la sua eredità pontificale* (Turin, 1939), is critical.

For Pius XII one should be sure to take note of the eulogy delivered by his close friend, Fr. Robert Leiber, S. J., "Pius XII," published in German in *Stimmen der Zeit: Monatschrift für das Geistesleben der Gegenwart* (163 Band-84 Jahrgang 1958/59—2 Heft; November 1958), pp. 81–100. For sympathetic assessments see also Alden Hatch and Seamus Walshe, *Crown of Glory: The Life of Pope Pius XII* (Garden City, N.Y., 1965); Oscar Halecki (in collaboration with James F. Murray), *Pius XII* (London, 1954); Nazareno Padellaro, *Portrait of Pius XII*, translated by Michael Derrick (London, 1956); Konstantin, Prince of Bavaria, *The Pope*, translated by Diana Pike (New York, 1956); Joseph F. Dinneen, *Pius XII: Pope of Peace* (New York, 1939); and Alexis Curvers' defensive *Pie XII: Le Pape outragé* (Paris, 1964). James W. Naughton, S. J., *Pius XII on World Problems* (New York, 1943), is a collection of various pronouncements by this pontiff. The anticlerical article by George La Piana, "The Political Heritage of Pius XII," in Frances Keene (ed.), *Neither Liberty Nor Bread* (New York, 1940), pp. 201–210, should be noted.

General works that seek to place the papacy in the historical context of the modern world include such sympathetic studies as Edward E. Y. Hales, *The Catholic Church in the Modern World: A Survey from the French Revolution to the Present* (New York, 1958); H. Daniel-Rops, *A Fight for God, 1870–1939*, Vol. IX of *History of the Church of Christ*, translated from the French by John Warrington (New York, 1966); Karl Otmar von Aretin, *The Papacy and the Modern World*, translated by Roland Hill (New York, 1970); Waldemar Gurian and M. A. Fitzsimons (eds.), *The Catholic Church in World Affairs* (Notre Dame, 1954); Joseph N. Moody (ed.), *Church and Society: Catholic Social and Political Thought and Movements, 1789–1950* (New York, 1953); Luigi Sturzo, *Church and State* (New York, 1939); Robert A. Graham, S. J., *Vatican Diplomacy: A Study of Church and State on the International Plane* (Princeton, 1959); and Jerome G. Kerwin, *Catholic*

Viewpoint on Church and State (New York, 1960). Much more critical, and in some cases frankly hostile, are Carlo Falconi, *The Popes in the Twentieth Century,* previously mentioned; John P. McKnight, *The Papacy: A New Appraisal* (New York and Toronto, 1952); Avro Manhattan, *The Catholic Church Against the Twentieth Century* (London, 1947), and *The Vatican in World Politics* (New York, 1949); Paul Blanshard, *Communism, Democracy, and Catholic Power* (Boston, 1951); the English foreign correspondent, Peter Nichols, *The Politics of the Vatican* (New York, 1968), ranging from Constantine to Paul VI; and Anthony Rhodes, *The Vatican in the Age of the Dictators, 1922–1945* (London, 1973).

A good many of the encyclicals that focused particularly on the political and social problems of the twentieth century and totalitarianism have been published in useful collections: Anne Fremantle (ed.), *The Papal Encyclicals in Their Historical Context* (New York, 1956); Francis J. Powers (ed.), *Papal Pronouncements on the Political Order* (Westminster, Md., 1952), covering the period 1878 to 1951; Sister Mary Claudia Carlen, *A Guide to the Encyclicals of the Roman Pontiffs from Leo XIII to the Present Day (1878–1939)* (New York, 1939); Oswald von Nell-Breuning, S. J., *Reorganization of Social Economy: The Social Encyclicals Developed and Explained* (Milwaukee, 1936–37); *Sixteen Encyclicals of His Holiness Pope Pius XI, 1926–1937* (Washington, 1938); Charles Paul Bruehl, *The Pope's Plan for Social Reconstruction: A Commentary on the Social Encyclicals of Pius XI* (New York, 1939); and Igino Giordani (ed.), *Le Encicliche sociali dei Papi da Pio IX a Pio XII (1864–1946)* (Rome, 1948).